KANSAS

KANSAS BY ROAD

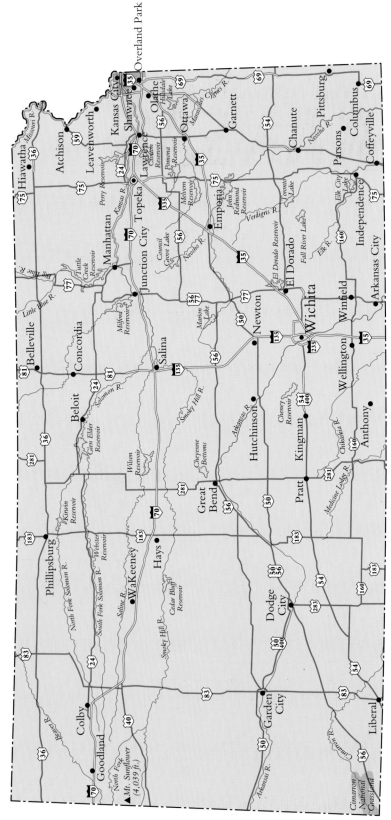

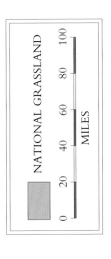

NATIONAL GRASSLAND

MILES

0   20   40   60   80   100

N
W   E
S

CELEBRATE THE STATES
KANSAS

Ruth Bjorklund

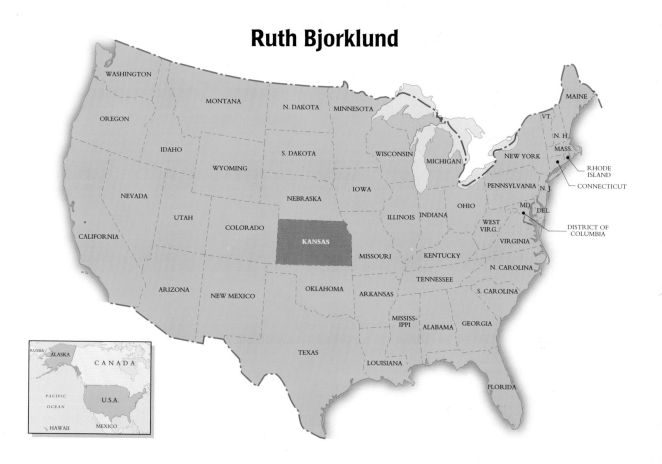

BENCHMARK BOOKS

MARSHALL CAVENDISH
NEW YORK

For Nana

Benchmark Books
Marshall Cavendish Corporation
99 White Plains Road
Tarrytown, New York 10591-9001

Library of Congress Cataloging-in-Publication Data
Bjorklund, Ruth.
Kansas / Ruth Bjorlund.
p. cm. — (Celebrate the states)
Includes bibliographical references and index.
Summary: Describes the geographic features, history, government, people,
and attractions of the state known as the Sunflower State.
ISBN 0-7614-0646-8 *601862774*
1. Kansas Juvenile literature. [1. Kansas.] I. Title. II. Series.
F681.3.B56   2000   978.1—dc21   99-16627   CIP

Maps and graphics supplied by Oxford Cartographers, Oxford, England

Photo Research by Candlepants Incorporated

Cover Photo: Michael C. Snell

The photographs in this book are used by permission and through the courtesy of; *Joel Sartore* : 6-7, 10-11,
70-71, 73, 76, 79,88-89, 109, 115. *Photo Researchers, Inc.*: Van Nostrand, 14(top); Jess R. Lee, 4(bottom);
Gary D. McMichael, 61; Keith Kent, 24; David R. Frazier, 67; Van Bucher, 68; Rod Planck, 123(right);Bonnie
Sue, 123(left); Leonard Lee Rue, 126(right) Sam Pierson Jr., 126(left). *Unicorn Stock Photos*: Aneal Vohra, 17,
76-77, 77, 78, 86, 110, 114, 119, 139; Eric R. Berndt, 59; Bob Barrett, 120. *The Image Bank*: Harald Sund,
21, 128, back cover; A.T. Wilett, 25; Weinberg-Clark, 64-65; *Spencer Museum of Art, The University of Kansas,
Gift of the Women's Club*: 26-27. *National Museum of American Art, Washington D.C./Art Resource, New York*: 29.
Kansas State Historical Society, Topeka, Kansas: 35, 37, 40, 44, 46, 47. *Archive Photos*: 36,132, 138; Carl T.
Gosset/New York Times Company, 92; Lee, 97; Herman Leonard, 136. *Corbis*: 32,95, 98, 101, 135; David
Muench, 13, 18; Bettmann, 49, 58,104, 133, 134,137; Lake County Museum, 42; Jim Sugar Photography,
50-51; Philip Gould, 83; Mitchell Gerber,131.*Bill Stephens*: 52-53, 81, 106-107, 117, 130. *Verna Lee Coleman* :
56. *Michael C. Snell, 63.The Menninger Foundation*: 91. *University of Kansas Sports Information*: 96. *Raytheon
Aircraft Corporation*: 102. *Office of the Secretary of State Kansas*: 122 (lower).

Printed in Italy

1   3   5   6   4   2

CONTENTS

KANSAS IS . . . .

Kansas is the place where land meets sky.

"The prairie path leads to the sky path; the paths are one: the continents are two; and you must make your journey from the prairies to the sky."　　　　　—William A. Quayle, author

It is rich in history . . .

"To the border wars succeeded hot winds, droughts, grasshoppers; and to the disasters of nature succeeded in turn the scourge of man . . . the whole history of the state was a series of disasters, and always something new, extreme, bizarre, until the name Kansas became a byword, a synonym for the impossible."
　　　　　　　　　　　　—Carl Becker, historian, 1910

"No other Territory has ever had such a history."
　—President Abraham Lincoln, in a speech at Elwood, Kansas, 1859

. . . and occupies a special place.

"Kansas is the navel of the nation."　　—John James Ingalls, author

Kansas welcomes some of us . . .

"Kansas is in a way a comforting presence—a reminder of a simpler America that not only was, but lives on." —Neal Peirce, journalist

. . . while putting off others.

"As I crossed the border, I settled upon a simple system for making Kansas just as interesting per hour as the average U.S. state. All you need is a car that goes 300 miles per hour."

—Philip Greenspun, scientist

Kansas is . . .

"An extraordinary, ordinary place."   —Neal Peirce, journalist

---

Kansas is often two things at once. Gentle, green, rolling hills run alongside jagged, rocky cliffs. Bountiful harvests are eaten by plagues of locusts. Floods follow droughts, the sun parches, and blizzards blind; yet people remain fiercely loyal to their state. Kansas-born author Kenneth S. Davis writes that he has "never met a Kansan anywhere whose heart wasn't buried in Kansas." Kansas is the geographic center of the United States, the heart of the nation's heartland. People speak proudly of the wide-open skies, of the far-reaching prairies, and of a history so alive it seems to be breathing. The spell that Kansas casts on its citizens is impossible to describe. Most say simply, "Kansas is a state of mind."

1 EAST MEETS WEST

The 82,282 square miles of Kansas plains, prairies, hills, valleys, canyons, cliffs, and sand dunes form one giant, tilting slab of earth. From roughly seven hundred feet above sea level in the southeastern corner of the state, Kansas rises steadily toward its highest point, 4,039-foot Mount Sunflower in the northwestern corner. At first glance, this almost perfectly rectangular state may appear flat and featureless. But the journey across swamps, deserts, badlands, and the vast High Plains is an eye-opener.

EASTERN KANSAS

There is abundant water in eastern Kansas. Two major rivers flow west to east, the Kansas in the north and the Arkansas in the south. The Missouri River winds along the state's northeast corner. Along its banks are marshes and thick, humid forests of elm, hickory, and cottonwood that shelter ducks, beaver, and woodland birds. The Missouri was a major thoroughfare for early traders and settlers, and depots and towns sprang up along it. Traveling the river today, you will pass three of the state's six largest cities.

Grasslands once extended from Canada to Texas and from Ohio to the Rocky Mountains. Farmers and ranchers turned so much of the grassland into cropland that little remains untouched. Too rocky to plow, eastern Kansas's Flint Hills contain the largest expanse of wild

In 1997, the Tallgrass Prairie National Preserve was created to protect some of Kansas's graceful grassland. At the dedication ceremony, former U.S. senator Nancy Kassebaum declared, "This is the most beautiful land in the world."

tallgrass left in the nation. Native American author William Least Heat-Moon writes that "the grasses can grow to 10 feet, high enough that the red man once stood atop their horses to see 20 yards ahead." In the Flint Hills, bluestem grasses, wildflowers, and limestone-and-flint-specked mesas are a refuge for a colorful array of prairie birds.

The greater prairie chicken is one of many birds that make their home amid Kansas grasses.

Small animals such as badgers are abundant in the Flint Hills.

CICADAS

There are millions of species of insects living in Kansas wheatfields, grasslands, and gardens. Some insects are helpful, some are pests, and some make headlines.

Cicadas are large insects that live most of their life burrowed in the ground. They only leave their hideaways to mate. Some come out after seven years, some after thirteen, and some after seventeen. Above ground, cicadas live on trees. Most years, their arrival is only briefly noticed. But when two or more cycles coincide, watch out!

Each group of cicadas makes their own chirp, and when there are two or more groups, their chirping becomes a pounding, daylong din. People can go a little crazy from the ceaseless noise. Insect expert George Byers calls it cicada-psychosis.

Once the cicadas mate, the adults die. When two or more groups mate in the same year, there are a lot of dead bodies laying about. In 1998, the thirteen-year and the seventeen-year cycles came together. "The carcasses were so plentiful you could scoop them off the ground with a bucket! Dogs love to eat them," laughs Lawrence gardener Marilyn Teeter. "My neighbor's dog ate so many he got sick and had to wear a muzzle!" Cicadas won't hurt you or your garden, but you'd better keep some earplugs handy!

Among them are the upland sandpiper, eastern meadowlark, and greater prairie chicken. Amid the prairie's forty species of grasses, many creatures rove, including badgers, foxes, bobcats, deer, and wild turkey.

South and east of the Flint Hills are colorful limestone and shale ridges called the Osage Cuestas. *Cuesta* is the Spanish word for "hillside." On one side the Osage Cuestas are steep and craggy, while on the other, tractors plow gentle, rolling fields.

Kansas's southeast corner is nothing like its image as a vast golden prairie. Densely forested, wet, and hilly, it is part of the Ozark Mountains, which extend south and east.

CENTRAL KANSAS

Venturing into central Kansas, you are reminded of the ancient seas that once covered the region. Though the water has disappeared, sandy beaches have endured. High winds have blown the sand into colossal dunes. "It's so sandy that when the pioneers first tried to irrigate their crops by building canals in their fields, the water in the canals drained out right through the sand!" laughs historian Barbara Brackman.

This is Arkansas River country (pronounced "Ar-KAN-sas" in this state). The Arkansas River begins high in the Colorado Rockies and sweeps grandly through southern Kansas in a giant arc. The center of the arc is called the Great Bend. Two incredible wetlands, Cheyenne Bottoms and Quivira National Wildlife Refuge, are located nearby. Although they may seem desolate to humans, these rich marshes play host to a teeming horde of waterfowl. In spring and fall, half of all North America's shorebirds stop to feed on tasty Kansas bloodworms. This feast attracts many of the nations' endangered and threatened birds, including peregrine falcons, bald eagles, whooping cranes, and piping plovers.

North and west beyond the Great Bend marshes, the land returns to rolling prairies and hills. The Smoky Hill River curves and meanders across the central plains. Sometimes, the river's course shifts and a section of it gets blocked off, forming a small, curved lake. Most of Kansas's natural lakes are these so-called oxbow lakes.

Throughout central Kansas are limestone deposits. One of the largest is in the Chalk Hills. Limestone is soft when it is underground, but once exposed to the air, it hardens. Because trees are rare in this part of Kansas, the resourceful pioneers used limestone

Millions of migrating birds stop off at Quivira National Wildlife Refuge each year.

The strange formations called Monument Rocks are a far cry from the typical image of Kansas.

as a building material. They carved limestone into fences, bridges, and barns, many of which are still in use today. Farther west, in the Kansas Badlands, solitary formations tower over the surrounding plains.

WESTERN KANSAS

If you dropped out of the sky, like Dorothy in *The Wizard of Oz*, and landed somewhere in Kansas and wanted to find your way home, you could begin by measuring the length of the wild grasses. If the grasses were long and lush, you would be in eastern Kansas; short and flat, you would be in the west.

Short, flat buffalo grass and tumbleweed sage are common in the High Plains of western Kansas. There is little water here. Winds hurl across the plains, and without trees or barriers, they pick up extraordinary speed. It should be no surprise that this is one of the least populated areas in the entire country. "It's so empty out here, if you see another person, you have to acknowledge it," explains a Scott County resident. "We do the two-fingered wave; that's your two forefingers lifted off the steering wheel."

THE STORY OF WATER

"In eastern Kansas, people debate water-quality issues. In western Kansas, people fight over who gets to use how much," says Charles Jones, who was once the state's director of environment. "In eastern Kansas, we're better off than we were ten years ago, and ten years from now, we should be better off still." But in western Kansas it seems the problems are just beginning.

More than ten thousand years ago, many rivers ran down from the Rocky Mountains and over the High Plains. The sand and gravel beds that make up the High Plains acted like a giant sponge soaking up the river water and storing it underground. Today, this underground water, called the Ogallala Aquifer, lies beneath a region extending from South Dakota to Texas. It is capable of holding a quadrillion gallons of water. This region averages only eighteen inches of rain a year, so the Ogallala Aquifer is the High Plains' main water source. Since pioneer days, people have been taking water out of the aquifer. "We say they are mining water," says Jones. "It's fossil water, historical water. If we drained it all, it would take six thousand years to replace."

In this region, wheat grows in seemingly endless rows. But some farm methods waste this precious water. Jones explains, "When you fly over the west you see those big green circles on the ground. That's center-pivot irrigation. With it, farmers can irrigate fields that aren't flat enough for irrigation pipes. Trouble is, those center pivots spray water all over the place. Most of it evaporates before it ever hits the ground." Farmers are currently using the water twenty-five times faster than it can be replaced. Many rivers, springs, and wetlands fed by the aquifer have gone dry. In places, even the Arkansas River has been reduced to a trickle. "We're really trying to come up with solutions," contends Jones. "We don't want to say 'no more,' but when the water is gone, it's gone. Farmers need to ask themselves, 'Is the value of the crop worth bringing up the water?'"

BLAZING HEAT AND BITTER COLD

"Everybody says, 'You don't like the weather, wait a minute!' Well, that's true. I once watched the temperature drop forty degrees in one afternoon," laughs one Lawrence resident. Temperatures in Kansas can range from arctic to broiling. As early as March and as late as

Scientists and farmers are working together to find ways to grow crops using less water.

October, it can be a blistering one hundred degrees. On the other hand, you could find yourself shivering in below-freezing weather in July. And when the snows come in winter, aided by blustery winds, it

LAND AND WATER

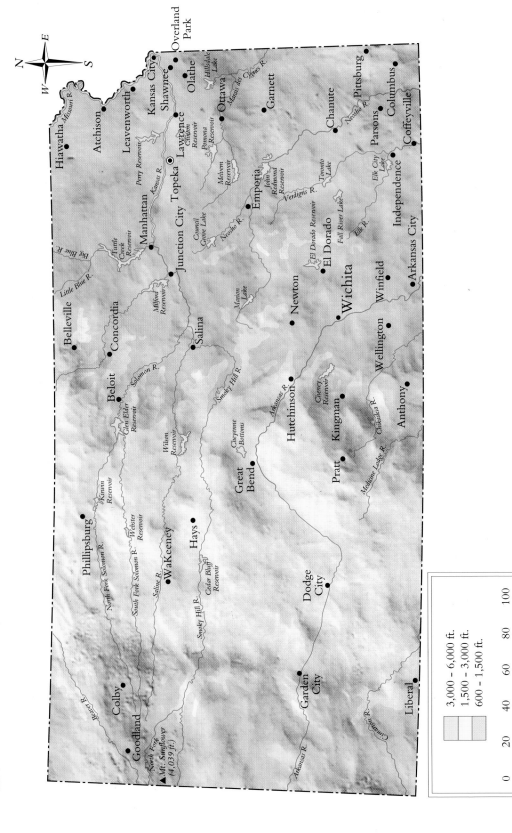

N E S W

Hiawatha
Missouri R.
Atchison
Leavenworth
Kansas City
Shawnee
Olathe
Overland Park
Hillsdale Lake
Ottawa
Marais des Cygnes R.
Garnett
Chanute
Pittsburg
Neosho R.
Columbus
Parsons
Coffeyville
Lawrence
Clinton Reservoir
Pomona Reservoir
Topeka
Kansas R.
Perry Reservoir
Manhattan
Melvern Reservoir
Emporia
John Redmond Reservoir
Verdigris R.
Toronto Lake
Elk City Lake
Independence
Junction City
Tuttle Creek Reservoir
Neosho R.
Council Grove Lake
Elk R.
Fall River Lake
Arkansas City
Big Blue R.
Little Blue R.
El Dorado Reservoir
El Dorado
Belleville
Concordia
Milford Reservoir
Salina
Marion Lake
Newton
Wichita
Winfield
Solomon R.
Beloit
Glen Elder Reservoir
Smoky Hill R.
Wellington
Wilson Reservoir
Cheyenne Bottoms
Hutchinson
Arkansas R.
Cheney Reservoir
Kingman
Chikaskia R.
Anthony
Phillipsburg
Kirwin Reservoir
North Fork Solomon R.
Webster Reservoir
South Fork Solomon R.
Saline R.
WaKeeney
Hays
Pratt
Medicine Lodge R.
Smoky Hill R.
Cedar Bluff Reservoir
Dodge City
Colby
Goodland
North Fork
▲Mt. Sunflower (4,039 ft.)
Beaver R.
Garden City
Arkansas R.
Cimarron R.
Liberal

MILES

0	20	40	60	80	100

3,000 – 6,000 ft.
1,500 – 3,000 ft.
600 – 1,500 ft.

is frigid. "They have gates on the turnpike and they just close the road straight through to the Rockies," says a High Plains resident. In the swirling snows, homesteaders sometimes tied a rope between their house and barn, fearing that they might otherwise lose their way and freeze to death. Despite winter's hardships, it was the heat of summer that forced tens of thousands of Kansas pioneers off their farms. Summer's achingly long, hot days often came without rain. Droughts parched fields and shriveled crops. Defeated, homesteaders returned east, the signs on their wagons reading, "In God We Trusted—In Kansas We Busted."

Kansas is one of the windiest states in the nation. Although the relentless wind can be troublesome, it has its positive side. Kansas businesswoman Leslie Hargis explains, "Whenever I travel to New York or L.A. and I see all the air pollution there that we don't have here, I come home and say to myself, 'I better stop cussin' the wind!'" It is fitting that the name Kansas comes from the Kansa tribe whose name means, "people of the south wind."

Kansas weather can be spectacular. Warm winds carrying moisture from the Gulf of Mexico collide with chilling blasts from the Arctic. Year-round, but especially in spring and fall, these weather fronts draw battlelines on the Kansas plains. A carefree, balmy day can suddenly be ripped apart by hail, lightning, and tornadoes. Western High Plains resident Angela Bates-Tomkins has seen many such storms, saying, "When a storm rolls up in Kansas, you never forget you're on Planet Earth!"

Kansans are used to challenges from nature. The state motto is "to the stars through difficulties." Tornadoes, dust storms, floods,

A BOLT FROM THE BLUE

"You haven't experienced anything unless you have been in a Kansas thunderstorm!" says High Plains resident Angela Bates-Tompkins.

Lightning & Thunderstorm Safety Tips:

• Take shelter as soon as you hear thunder. Lightning can strike miles away from the storm clouds. This is called a "bolt from the blue."
• Don't be caught on a ballfield, golf course, boat, or in an open vehicle.
• Stay inside a house, building, or car (electricity will travel around the outside).
• Don't use a corded telephone or other appliances. Lightning can pass through the wires. ("My phone once melted," says Bates-Tompkins.)
• Stay away from windows.
• Don't take a bath or wash dishes by hand. Lightning can follow the metal water pipes. ("I used to have a metal frame bed," recalls Bates-Tompkins, "but when it stormed, I slept on the sofa!")

Dramatic storm clouds menace the Kansas prairie.

droughts, lightning, hail, blizzards—all can bring tragedy. Yet for more than two-thirds of the year, the sun shines overhead in a crystal-clear, blue Kansas sky.

2 A TIMELESS LAND

Redfield Panorama, by Robert Sudlow

Eons ago, Kansas was a watery home to prehistoric sea life. But once the seas disappeared, Kansas became a windswept stage for some of the liveliest events in American history.

THE FIRST PEOPLE

The first humans arrived in Kansas about 13,000 years ago. These people, called Paleo-Indians, hunted large animals such as the woolly mammoth, the forerunner of the elephant, and gathered nuts, roots, and berries. They were nomadic people who moved about, carrying all their belongings with them.

Later came another people known as the Mound Builders because they buried their dead in large dirt mounds. They formed permanent villages of dwellings made with woven grass and poles. The Mound Builders were Kansas's first farmers. They planted corn and squash in their fields. They also made pottery and tools.

By the 1500s, descendants of the Mound Builders called the Wichita lived in Kansas, as did the Pawnee. The Wichita used poles and woven grass "shingles" to construct cone-shaped lodges, while the Pawnee made lodges of earth and compressed grasses. Women tended fields of corn and other crops, while the men hunted. Their most valued prey was buffalo. When on the hunting trail, they lived in tepees made of buffalo skins. This life was akin to that of the

This painting by George Catlin shows the grass lodges in which the Wichita Indians lived.

Kaw and Osage tribes who later moved into eastern Kansas. The Plains Apache followed herds of buffalo across western Kansas. In the 1700s, the Comanche moved onto the Plains Apache territory. The Comanche raided other tribes. They were the most feared of all the tribes, because they rode horses, which made them swifter and more powerful than warriors afoot.

EUROPEANS ARRIVE

In 1541, the first Europeans found their way to Kansas. Spanish explorers from Mexico had made forays north searching for a legendary kingdom of gold. In present-day New Mexico, a Native American slave called El Turco, who hoped to return to his home in the central plains, convinced explorer Francisco Vásquez de Coronado that he knew where to find such a kingdom. He called it Quivira. For forty-two days the Spaniards tramped across the High Plains, searching for Quivira. After thundering across the Arkansas River and confronting an encampment of Wichita Indians, Coronado at last came to a halt. Looking around at the simple farms, Coronado realized that the Wichita did not dwell in a city of gold. Disappointed, he turned back.

As news of his exploits spread, other Spanish explorers and missionaries ventured into the area. In 1673, the first French explorers arrived from Canada. Interested in furs, they happily discovered beaver and bison and began trading with the Osage and Pawnee. For more than one hundred years, Spain and France fought over what would become Kansas. Finally, in 1803, President Thomas Jefferson persuaded France to sell its land west of the Mississippi River, including Kansas, to the United States. The sale was called the Louisiana Purchase, and it doubled the size of the nation.

ENTER THE AMERICANS

Many Americans on the East Coast didn't care about the western frontier. A Boston newspaper reported that it was "a waste, a wilderness unpeopled by anything but wolves and wandering Indians." But Jefferson disagreed. He was eager to explore the new territory and commissioned a "Corps of Discovery" led by Meriwether Lewis and William Clark to collect information about its land and people. In 1804, they set out from St. Louis, Missouri, bound for the Pacific Ocean. Although their stay in Kansas was brief, they recorded news of "beautiful plains that were breathtaking." Two years later, Lieutenant Zebulon Pike was sent to the Great Plains to keep peace with the Indians. Pike reported, "These vast plains of the western hemisphere may become in time as celebrated as the sandy deserts of Africa."

Pike's report influenced mapmakers, who labeled the Great Plains "the Great American Desert." The U.S. Secretary of War John C. Calhoun used this information to determine Kansas "unfit for cultivation." He thought it would be a good place to relocate the Native Americans living in the East, where white settlers had been clamoring for more land. So, in 1830, Congress enacted the Indian Removal Bill, which forced twenty-seven eastern tribes west into Kansas. The Indians would live in Kansas forever, the government declared. Kansas was the "permanent Indian frontier."

It was not permanent for long. White settlers continued advancing on the frontier. The Santa Fe Trail, from Franklin, Missouri, to Santa Fe, in what is now New Mexico, was a major trading route stretching across Kansas. The Oregon Trail passed through

Prospectors streamed across Kansas on the Overland Trail after miners struck gold in California.

Kansas's northeastern corner. And when gold was discovered in California in 1848, thousands of hopeful prospectors traversed Kansas on the Overland Trail. Between gold seekers, traders, and pioneers, more and more white settlers encountered Kansas. Some noted that the soil was actually very fertile. They demanded that the Kansas Territory be opened to homesteading. In 1854, the government passed the Kansas-Nebraska Act, permitting whites to settle in Kansas.

BLEEDING KANSAS

The Kansas-Nebraska Act made way for more than homesteading. It also opened the door to bloodshed and bitter rivalry. The act declared that Kansas had to choose whether to allow slavery. At the time, Congress had as many members from Southern slave states as it did from Northern free states, and sessions often ended in deadlock. Each side wanted Kansas to vote with them. The choice Kansas voters made would influence the entire nation.

Proslavery groups, called Bushwackers, and antislavery abolitionists, called Jayhawks, fought viciously in Kansas. To thwart the Free State movement, Bushwackers crossed into Kansas from Missouri and voted illegally for proslavery laws. When abolitionists heard of this, hundreds migrated to Kansas to fight back. One of the most fanatical was John Brown. Abolitionists were usually nonviolent, but John Brown had had enough. He and his sons led many raids on proslavery settlements. Until his death in 1859, Brown fought to free slaves. Violence so ruled Kansas during this period that it became known as Bleeding Kansas.

Kansas finally entered the Union as a free state on January 29, 1861. But that did not mean the bloodshed had ended. The Civil War erupted two months later. Taking up the Southern, or Confederate, cause was Lawrence resident William Quantrill. After joining the Confederate army in Missouri, Quantrill decided the Confederate troops were not aggressive enough. Set on terrorizing Kansas, he organized a band of raiders that included legendary outlaws Cole Younger and Frank and Jesse James. On August 21, 1863, Quantrill led three hundred proslavery thugs on a raid against the city of

QUANTRELL

William C. Quantrill ("Quantrell") was a Confederate raider. A cold-hearted killer, he and his "border bandits," including outlaws Jesse and Frank James and Cole Younger, wreaked havoc during the Civil War. On August 21, 1863, after sacking several small towns along the Kansas-Missouri border, they rode into Lawrence, where they burned down some 200 buildings and killed more than 150 residents.

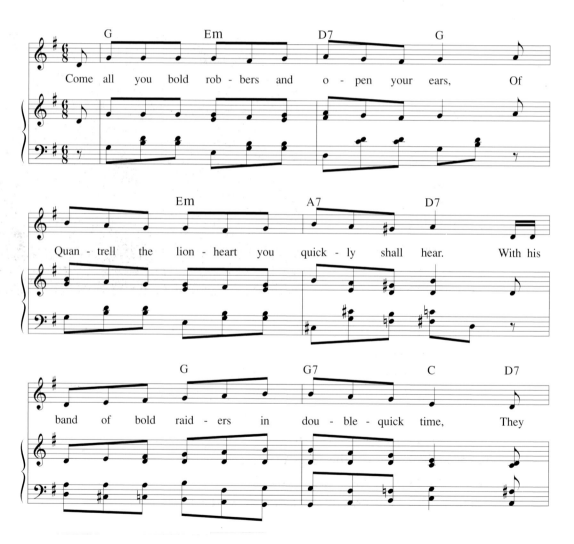

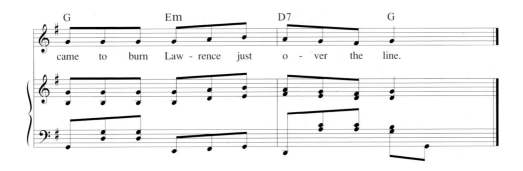

came to burn Law - rence just o - ver the line.

Chorus:
All routing and shouting
  and giving the yell,
Like so many demons
  just raised up from Hell,
The boys they were drunken
  with powder and wine,
And came to burn Lawrence
  just over the line.

They came to burn Lawrence, they came not to stay,
They rode in one morning at breaking of day.
Their guns were a-waving and horses a-foam,
And Quantrell was riding his famous big roan. *Chorus*

They came to burn Lawrence, they came not to stay,
Jim Lane he was up at the break of the day.
He saw them a-coming and got in a fright,
Then crawled in a corncrib to get out of sight. *Chorus*

In 1855, John Brown headed for Kansas to fight the proslavery forces there.

Lawrence. They murdered more than 150 men and burned two hundred homes and businesses to the ground. It was one of the largest civilian massacres ever in the United States.

By the time the Confederates surrendered in 1865, more than 20,000 Kansans had served in the Union army, more in proportion to population than any other state.

FRONTIER LIFE

After the Civil War, Americans resumed their westward expansion. For a ten-dollar fee, any citizen could be granted 160 acres. Thousands of veterans and freed slaves came to claim land. Despite the hardships and uncertainties, the homesteaders believed the West was the land of opportunity.

Pioneers first found shelter in crude tents or in their wagons. But once they suffered their first Kansas storm, they realized a sturdy house was not just a luxury. Since there were few trees with which to build a home, the pioneers had to be inventive. Watching their plows churn up long, hard chunks of earth, they found a solution.

The Mead family built their dugout house into a hill near Bloom, Kansas.

By chopping the earth, or sod, into blocks they could build a sod house, or soddy. For a roof, they often used topsoil. You could guess how long a soddy had been standing by the height of the wild grass and sunflowers that sprouted on the roof. Some soddies were simply a single wall in front of a dwelling carved into the side of a hill. This type was quicker to build but was more dangerous because sometimes a stray steer would wander across the "roof" and crash through on the family below!

Soddies were everywhere. Leaky and cold in winter, and rodent-infested year-round, they were still beloved by grateful pioneers. Of her soddy, pioneer Lydie Lyons wrote, "The wind whistled through the walls in winter and the dust blew in summer, but we papered the walls with newspapers and made rag carpets for the floor, and we thought we were living well."

The prairie wind was responsible for another common sight on the Kansas frontier, the windmill. It was a rare homestead that could boast a pond, stream, or river nearby, so pioneers dug deep wells for water. The pumps bringing water to the surface were powered by windmills. In Kansas, you couldn't count on much from one day to the next, but you could count on the wind.

WILD AND WOOLLY

In the 1860s, the railroads surged westward. Tracks were laid from one end of Kansas to the other, changing the prairie forever. The first to suffer were the bison. For thousands of years, Plains Indians had coexisted with their prey. Native people respected the bison, which they depended on for their livelihood. When they killed,

TRUE GRIT

Pioneer families homesteaded Kansas as a team. Men and women shared equally the enormous challenges of conquering the prairie. Esther Clark's parents were pioneers. In her diary, she writes about the strength of her mother, Allena.

Mother has always been the gamest one of us. I can remember her hanging onto the reins of a runaway mule team, her black hair tumbling out of its pins and over her shoulders, her face set and white while one small girl clung with chattering teeth to the sides of the rocking wagon and a baby sister bounced about on the floor in paralyzed wonder. But, I think, as much courage as it took to hang onto the reins that day, it took more to live twenty-four hours at a time, month in and month out, on the lonely and lovely prairie, without giving up.

they wasted nothing. They used the bison's flesh, skin, and bones for meat, fuel, shelter, clothing, blankets, weapons, and utensils. But when the whites killed, it was only for food or sport. The railroads hired professional bison hunters like "Buffalo" Bill Cody to supply their crews with food. And no sooner were the railroads complete than thrill seekers hopped on board and took advantage of the easy targets. With shotguns aimed out windows, sport hunters spewed buckshot into herds of bison, leaving the carcasses to rot along the tracks. Before white settlement, 30 million bison roamed the plains. By 1890, they were nearly extinct.

Without the buffalo to sustain them, the area's Native Americans began to starve. The Indians who had not already been displaced

During the 1860s, the railroads ran special trains to bring sportsmen to the plains to shoot buffalo. They killed so many that the number of buffalo dropped from the millions to fewer than a thousand.

by the U.S. government started leaving Kansas for tribal lands in Oklahoma and Texas.

Meat was scarce in the eastern cities after the Civil War, but millions of wild Texas longhorn cattle roamed the Texas Panhandle. Once railroads were built as far west as Kansas, cattle could be shipped to eastern markets. Cowboys in Texas rounded up the longhorns and drove them up the Chisolm, Western, and Shawnee Trails to depots and stockyards in Abilene, Dodge City, Wichita,

Ellsworth, and the like. Money and men poured in. Almost overnight, the Kansas "cow towns" became boomtowns. Drawn by the lure of adventure, men and boys came from all over the country to become cowboys. Cattle drives were dusty, lonely, and treacherous, but once the cowboys brought the cattle to market, rowdy celebrations erupted. One journalist in Ellsworth reported, "Here you see in the streets men from every state and from almost every nation—the tall, long-haired Texas herder with his heavy jingling spurs and pair of six shooters; the gambler from all parts of the country, looking for unsuspecting prey; the honest immigrant in search of a homestead in the great free west; the keen stockbuyers; the wealthy Texas drovers; deadbeats; pickpockets; and horse thieves."

The rough-and-tumble lawlessness of Kansas cow towns produced some of the West's most famous lawmen and gunfighters. Wild Bill Hickok, Wyatt Earp, Bat Masterson, and Doc Holliday were all Kansas gunslingers.

TAMING THE WEST

"Barbed wire tamed the west," says one Kansas historian. Since the region had few trees, fences were rare. Although the longhorn ate well on the open range, their meat was stringy, and ranchers wanted to raise tastier breeds. But without fences they couldn't corral their herds. Then, in the 1870s barbed wire was invented. Using the twisted lengths of sharp metal, ranchers could section off grassland cheaply and rein in their valuable livestock.

As new breeds of cattle were developed, new crops were grown

THE REAL WILD WEST

"We're the real Wild West!" declares Kansas historian Barbara Brackman. "Think about all the images Hollywood has created about the West. Outlaws, cattle drives, cowboys, Pony Express riders, gunslingers, frontier forts . . . they all belong to Kansas!"

It's true.

Look at a map of Kansas and read the famous trail names: Chisholm, Oregon, Overland, Shawnee, Santa Fe. And when the cowboys rode into town to sell their cattle, buy supplies and whoop and holler, where did they go? Abilene, Ellsworth, Cimarron, Wichita, and Dodge City. Think of the historic forts: Hays, Riley, Larned, Scott, and Leavenworth. Or the legendary lawmen who kept the peace: Wyatt Earp, marshall of Wichita and Dodge City; Bat Masterson, Ford County sheriff; Wild Bill Hickok, marshall of Abilene; and Doc Holliday, dentist and deputy in Dodge City. And surely you have heard of Buffalo Bill Cody, the Pony Express rider, buffalo hunter, and Wild West Show promoter from Leavenworth, and Nat Love, known

as Deadwood Dick, the African-American cowboy from Dodge City? Lastly, think of all the infamous bad guys who attacked unsuspecting Kansans: the Dalton, James, and Younger Gangs, Quantrill's Raiders, and John Wesley Hardin.

"Cowboy boots," insists Brackman. "What better symbol of the true West than boots. And where were they made? Kansas! All the cowboys waited to get their boots in Dodge City or Abilene. Why, they still make the best ones in Olathe, Kansas, the 'Cowboy Boot Capital of the World!'"

Buffalo Bill Cody

to feed them. The Mennonites, a religious group that immigrated to Kansas from Russia, had brought with them a remarkable wheat called Turkey Red. Unlike other grains, this was a winter wheat that was planted in the fall and harvested in the spring before the harsh, dry summer set in. "Turkey Red" thrived in Kansas. Flour mills were built, and Kansas's farmers and ranchers began changing their state's nickname from the Great American Desert to America's Breadbasket.

Dependence on ranching and farming meant living at the mercy of ever-unpredictable Mother Nature. Kansas farmers lived through cycles of boom and bust. The 1870s brought good rains and harvests, but also a plague of locusts.

Grasshoppers and locusts are closely related. Grasshoppers are harmless, solitary, and stick close to home. But every once in a while, they use up their food supply, become excited, develop wings, and swarm. Once they are able to fly long distances, they are called locusts. A swarm of locusts sometimes covers fifteen square miles! In 1874, the locusts came, stunning the pioneers. One homesteader wrote that the swarm was "so thick you couldn't see the sun." Pioneer women watched in astonishment as the hoppers ate the wash on their line and the boards off their houses. One looked on in horror as "the hoppers came inside, eating all the food in the cupboards, the tool handles and furniture." The locusts' dying bodies poisoned the water; the air was filled with their smell. Chickens and hogs that ate the bodies tasted so much like the hoppers they couldn't be eaten. Kansas set up a relief committee for the victims of the plague and nearly went bankrupt trying to help, so great was the damage.

But the worst was yet to come. According to writer Mark Twain, the 1880s and 1890s were a "time in America when the rich got richer and the poor, poorer." The railroads gouged farmers with high shipping fees, and banks charged high interest on loans. Farmers cried foul. First they joined the Grange or the Farmer's Alliance. In these groups, farmers tried to form a united front against low crop prices and unfair costs. Later, they formed their own political party, the People's, or Populist, Party. Populists

In the late nineteenth century, mills sprang up across Kansas to process Kansas's flourishing wheat crop.

wanted protection from the railroads and banks. They accused the government of favoring rich corporations. The Populist Party passed many important reforms, such as child labor laws, a shortened workday, and new banking laws. Twice Kansans elected Populists to the office of governor.

WARS AND DEPRESSION

When the United States entered World War I in 1917, Kansans rallied in support of their country. Their battle cry was "Win the War with Wheat!" Tractors and plows turned more and more buffalo grass into cropland. Schoolchildren were encouraged to help farmers at harvesttime. The army trained soldiers at Fort Leavenworth and other Kansas posts. People sacrificed with "meatless Tuesdays" and "wheatless Wednesdays." Kansas was feeding the world and mining coal, oil, and helium in an all-out war effort.

After the war, the 1920s saw trucks, tractors, and combines replace plows and horses in the fields. Electricity was reaching out to rural areas, and everyone seemed to be buying Henry Ford's automobile. People were happy with their new mobility. For $295 you could buy a car and drive up to forty miles an hour! Kansas oil fields grew richer as the automobile grew more popular.

But by the end of the decade, trouble was brewing. The stock market crashed in 1929, throwing the country into the Great Depression. Many people lost everything they owned. Wealth in land and wheat kept Kansas from falling as hard and as fast as the rest of the country. When the state finally came undone it was not from bad investments but from nature. Four rainless years in the

During World War I, thousands of acres of grassland in Kansas were plowed under so wheat could be planted.

early 1930s dried up all the moisture in the ground. So much grassland had been plowed under during the war effort that no vegetation remained to hold the soil in place. Dirt swirled in what people called black blizzards. The powdery soil collected against buildings and covered roads. People stuffed rugs and blankets around their doors and windows to keep the dust at bay. During one rare shower the air was so full of dirt that it rained mudballs. Many people left Kansas during the Dust Bowl era, as the wind yanked their livelihood away.

Then, in 1941, the country again went to war. Recruits from all over the nation were trained at army bases in Kansas. Metal manufacturing, aircraft production, and bumper crops of soybeans and grains were some of the contributions made by the state's hard-

During the Dust Bowl era, winds carried Kansas topsoil as far as five hundred miles out to sea.

working men and women. While news of World War II battles crackled over every radio, it was General Dwight D. Eisenhower, a Kansas farmboy, who led the armed forces in Europe. When he returned home to Abilene after the war, he found a state brimming with renewed hope. Kansas was building dams to prevent floods, new agricultural methods were being tried out, music, theater, and other arts were blooming. Said the general, "the proudest thing I can say today is that I'm from Abilene."

Americans came home from war and turned toward building a strong economy and a healthy society. There was much to do. Some Kansans were involved in one of the most significant events of the period. In 1951, eight-year-old Linda Brown lived in a racially mixed Topeka neighborhood. To get to school, Linda's white neighbors walked a few pleasant blocks to Sumner Elementary. But Linda and her African-American neighbors had to walk almost two miles from their home, crossing Topeka's busiest streets and a large railroad yard, in order to attend Monroe Elementary, a school for students who were not white. Linda's father and twelve other angry parents sued the Topeka Board of Education.

Thurgood Marshall, who later became the first African-American U.S. Supreme Court justice, was their attorney. He argued that separate, or segregated, schools for different races violated the Fourteenth Amendment to the Constitution, which guarantees all citizens "equal protection under the laws." The U.S. Supreme Court agreed in a landmark decision in 1954 known as *Brown* vs. *Board of Education of Topeka*. They ruled, "education . . . is a right which must be made available to all. . . . Separate educational facilities are inherently [by nature] unequal."

When the Supreme Court announced its decision ending school segregation, Thurgood Marshall recalled, "I was so happy I was numb."

Linda Brown's family and neighbors had changed the course of history. Through their courage and Marshall's brilliant arguments, segregation in schools was declared unconstitutional.

In recent decades, Kansas has undergone much change, while in some ways staying much the same. The state is an important player in the global economy, shipping wheat measured in hun-

dreds of millions of bushels around the world. Wichita produces more personal and military aircraft than anyplace else in the country. Oil wells keep pumping, minerals are mined, people leave their homes for jobs in the cities, and through it all, nature still has its

Two-thirds of Kansas's record-setting wheat crop goes toward feeding the world.

way. Tornadoes, hailstorms, blizzards, floods, and droughts have made headlines in America's Breadbasket for more than two hundred years. But whatever adversity Kansans may encounter, their spirit continues to lead them toward prosperity.

3 WORKING COMMUNITIES

The capitol in Topeka

Although Kansans have always been an independent lot, they have nonetheless agreed on the need for a just form of government laws. Even before Kansas was a state, the territory had a constitution protecting citizens' rights and providing for the common good.

INSIDE GOVERNMENT

The Kansas Constitution is similar to the U.S. Constitution in that it divides government into three branches: executive, legislative, and judicial.

Executive. The head of state in Kansas is the governor. He or she prepares the budget and approves or rejects proposed laws. Other elected executive branch officials include the lieutenant governor, the secretary of state, and the attorney general. All executive officials serve four-year terms.

Legislative. The Kansas legislature is made up of a house of representatives and a senate. The house has 125 members elected to two-year terms and the senate, 40 members elected to four-year terms. Once most members of both houses approve a proposed law, or bill, it is sent to the governor. The governor may sign the bill into law or veto it, which makes the bill invalid.

Judicial. The Kansas court system is divided into a supreme court, a court of appeals, district courts, and municipal courts. The

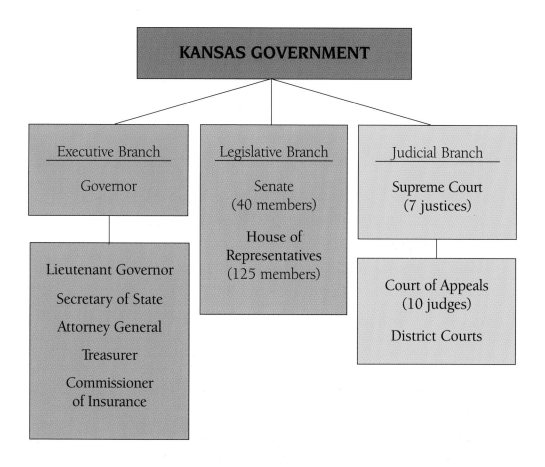

KANSAS GOVERNMENT

Executive Branch

Governor

Lieutenant Governor

Secretary of State

Attorney General

Treasurer

Commissioner
of Insurance

Legislative Branch

Senate
(40 members)

House of
Representatives
(125 members)

Judicial Branch

Supreme Court
(7 justices)

Court of Appeals
(10 judges)

District Courts

supreme court is the state's highest court. The decisions of the seven supreme court justices have authority over all the others. The governor selects supreme court justices from a list of nominations provided by a committee of lawyers. Once appointed, a justice must be reelected by voters every six years. District courts hear most of the state's cases. Those who are dissatisfied with a district court ruling, can ask for another trial. Most of these "appeals" are heard in the court of appeals, although some serious ones are heard by the supreme court. The supreme court can also review cases heard by the court of appeals. Municipal courts are city courts, which handle minor crimes such as traffic violations. But for all judges, their duty is the same—to interpret laws made by the legislature and to apply the laws fairly.

CITIZENS STAND TALL

"Kansans are independent thinkers," says historian Barbara Brackman. In 1887, years before most of the rest of the nation, Kansas men gave women the right to vote in local elections. As a result, women in Argonia, Kansas, voted for the first time alongside their brothers, husbands, fathers, and sons and elected Susanna Madora Salter the first female mayor in the country. Kansas was also the first

Susanna Madora Salter was the first woman in America to be elected mayor of a city.

state in the Union to ratify the Fifteenth Amendment to the Constitution, which granted voting rights to African-American men.

CRIME AND PREVENTION

In 1992, Meade County, Kansas, reported zero crimes for the year. While the rest of the state cannot boast such a distinction, its crime rate is lower than the national average. "The key to control is prevention," says a Garden City police officer. "It's important how community police handle things. We have no tolerance for gangs." Adolescent drug and alcohol abuse prevention programs are very visible across the state.

Kansas has long fought alcohol abuse. Many citizens from the late 1880s onward supported Prohibition, or the banning of liquor. Carry Nation of Medicine Lodge, Kansas, was famous for her activism. The widow of an alcoholic husband, she knew firsthand the curses of "Demon Rum." Brandishing a giant pickax, she slashed her way into saloons demanding that the men stop drinking. Though she was arrested for her vandalism, many women followed her lead in fighting for Prohibition. In part because of their efforts, in 1920, the United States passed the Eighteenth Amendment to the Constitution, prohibiting the manufacture and sale of alcohol. Prohibition was short-lived. It ended in 1933 because legislators believed it was responsible for government corruption, gangs, and a higher crime rate. Despite the rest of the country's change of heart, Kansas did not repeal its state prohibition on alcohol until 1948. Today, the state's alcohol consumption is less than half the national average. Carry Nation's influence lives on.

Carry Nation's battle against liquor had a lasting effect in Kansas. Even today, more than half the state's counties are still "dry," meaning they do not allow alcohol to be served in public places.

HOG POLITICS

One issue dividing Kansans today is swine. "Hogs are hot around here," says one Great Bend resident. Actually, they are "hot" all around Kansas and the Midwest. Hog farms owned by large corporations have been moving into traditional family farming areas. In Kansas, it "has pitted neighbor against neighbor," says a waitress in Jetmore, "cousin against cousin!" A typical family hog farm may raise a few hundred hogs, but the corporate farms rear five to ten thousand hogs at once.

People who welcome the corporate farms believe they will see more jobs and money coming into their towns. Opponents fear the environmental damage the pigs could do. Hog waste is stored in large lagoons where it carries bacteria that can seep into the groundwater or flow into nearby streams. Odor is another serious concern.

Some of the noisiest debates in the Kansas legislature in recent years have been over regulating corporate hog farms.

"Some corporations in other states haven't been good land stewards," says Al Silverstein of Great Bend. "We see their mistakes and say, 'How can we do it different?'" Silverstein advises, "Don't think of it as 'freaky environmentalists' versus mighty corporations, either. Environmentalists are very mainstream individuals these days. Everybody wants good water quality, clean air, and to protect our land. Farmers care a great deal about protecting their soil. The land is their factory."

In Great Bend, four city council members who supported the corporate hog industry were voted out of office. And in Jetmore, where bumper stickers proclaimed, "People vote . . . Hogs don't," citizens voted not to allow a corporate hog farm to locate there. Controversy over the hog farms will likely continue for years.

KANSAS WORKS

Kansas is a leading agricultural state. The state produces enough wheat to provide every person on Earth with six loaves of bread—more than 35 billion loaves!

But change is coming to Kansas farmers. "It's getting harder and harder to support a large family off of one farm," says Great Bend's Al Silverstein. "Look at how big those giant four-wheel drive tractors are, and how expensive! The small farm can't afford a $150,000 tractor and the big farm needs less workers because of it."

In 1996, Senator Pat Roberts of Kansas sponsored a farm bill in the U.S. Congress nicknamed the Freedom to Farm bill. Historically, the government paid farmers to grow what they asked them to

Kansas produces more wheat than any other state in the nation.

grow, and if the crops failed or if prices were too low, the government helped farmers out with payments called subsidies. The Freedom to Farm bill takes away those subsidies by the year 2002. It also allows farmers to grow whatever they want and however much of it they want. Since the law passed, farmers have grown so much wheat that there is a glut in the market and prices have fallen too low to make money. "They've taken the fun out of farming," mourns one Hodgeman County farmer. "You just can't get the prices you

EARNING A LIVING

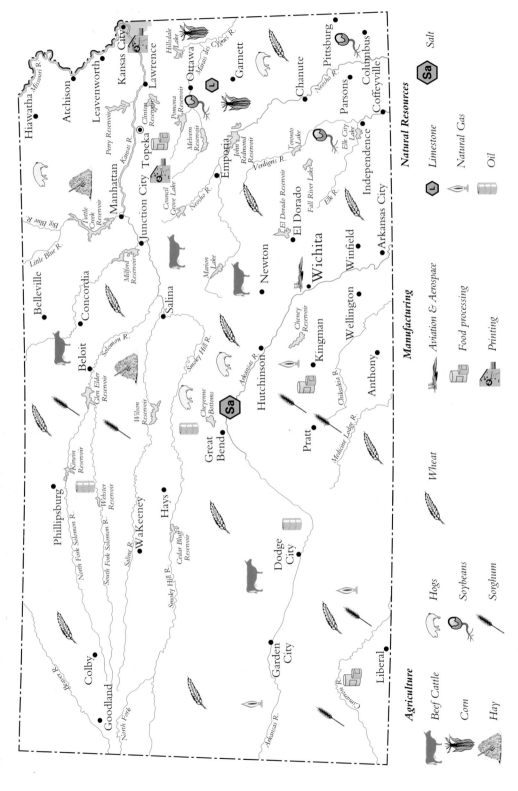

Natural Resources

Sa Salt
L Limestone
Natural Gas
Oil

Manufacturing

Aviation & Aerospace
Food processing
Printing

Agriculture

Beef Cattle
Corn
Hay
Hogs
Soybeans
Sorghum
Wheat

Hiawatha
Atchison
Leavenworth
Kansas City
Lawrence
Ottawa
Garnett
Chanute
Pittsburg
Columbus
Parsons
Coffeyville
Independence
Arkansas City
Winfield
Wichita
El Dorado
Newton
Emporia
Topeka
Junction City
Manhattan
Belleville
Concordia
Beloit
Salina
Hutchinson
Great Bend
Pratt
Kingman
Anthony
Wellington
Phillipsburg
WaKeeney
Hays
Dodge City
Garden City
Liberal
Colby
Goodland

Missouri R.
Big Blue R.
Little Blue R.
Kansas R.
Perry Reservoir
Clinton Reservoir
Pomona Reservoir
Melvern Reservoir
Marais des Cygnes R.
Hillsdale Lake
Neosho R.
Verdigris R.
John Redmond Reservoir
Toronto Lake
Elk City Lake
Fall River Lake
Elk R.
El Dorado Reservoir
Council Grove Lake
Tuttle Creek Reservoir
Milford Reservoir
Solomon R.
Glen Elder Reservoir
Wilson Reservoir
Smoky Hill R.
Cheyenne Bottoms
Arkansas R.
Cheney Reservoir
Chikaskia R.
Medicine Lodge R.
Kirwin Reservoir
Webster Reservoir
North Fork Solomon R.
South Fork Solomon R.
Saline R.
Smoky Hill R.
Cedar Bluff Reservoir
North Fork
Arkansas R.
Cimarron R.
Republican R.

KANSAS STATE FAIR

No festival draws more crowds, pleases more people, or shows off the state better than the Kansas State Fair in Hutchinson each September. "September is our beautiful month," says Kansan Nade Dangerfield, "and the fair is a slice of life not to be missed."

The wheat harvest in Kansas is in the spring, not autumn, but the state fair nonetheless displays Kansas's fruitful bounty. From the longest ear of corn (a recent winner was eleven inches) to 1,200 wheat entries, four-hundred-pound pumpkins, and exhibits of quilts, flowers, toy robots, photography, computers for use in tractors, Watusi goats, llamas, ostriches, buffalo, milking barns, big-name rock stars, and pig races, there really is something to amuse just about anyone. From the carnival rides to foods as diverse as Indian tacos and Amish sour cream raisin pie, a day at the fair is a memorable experience.

New and very popular is the Kansas State University School of Veterinary Medicine's Birthing Center. Fairgoers can watch calves, piglets, and chicks being born, and possibly have the chance to hold one of the newborns. Said one sixth-grade teacher from Wichita who brought his class to the birthing center, "None of my kids plan to be vets. We just came to watch. It's really incredible! A great field trip!"

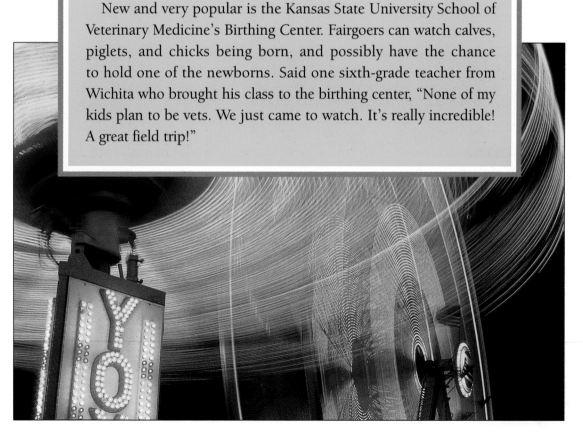

need." He is not alone. Many critics now call the law Freedom to Fail. Some farmers are now looking into new crops and growing methods. Silverstein declares, "It's a hardworking industry. There's solutions out there and we're working on them!"

When you think of Kansas, you think of wheat, or corn, or cattle. But as much as Kansas is a major supplier of these products, many more people head for jobs in the city than work on farms. Fewer than

Although more than 90 percent of Kansas is farmland, the vast majority of its citizens live and work in cities such as Wichita.

10 percent of Kansas's workers are employed on farms. And it is expected that farms will employ even fewer people in the years to come. The fastest-growing occupations in the state are in manufacturing, construction, and services.

Wichita is often called the Air Capital of the World. As early as 1908, planes were being built in Kansas. Aviators from all over the world were attracted to the activity in Wichita. The uncluttered

GROSS STATE PRODUCT: $80 BILLION

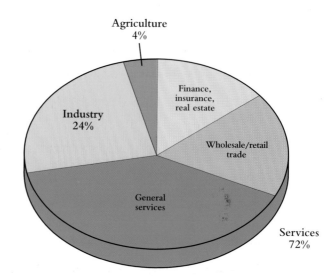

Agriculture
4%

Finance,
insurance,
real estate

Industry
24%

Wholesale/retail
trade

General
services

Services
72%

(2000 estimated)

countryside was perfect for experiments in flight. It was an exciting time, though not everything was smooth sailing. After landing in a pasture one pilot sent this telegraph message: "Motor cut. Forced landing. Hit cow. Cow died. Scared me." Cows today have little to fear from unexpected aircraft landings; they graze in safety far from the state's largest city.

Today, Wichita leads the nation in the production of business and military planes. More private aircraft are produced there than anywhere else in the world. Together, Boeing, Raytheon, Cessna, and Learjet employ about 35,000 people in the area, making Wichita's aerospace industry the state's largest employer.

The Coleman Company, whose coolers keep our soda cold, got its start in 1900 renting oil lamps to miners. Today, it employs thousands of Wichita workers. Pizza Hut also began in Wichita. In 1958, two college-aged brothers started their first restaurant with six hundred dollars borrowed from their mother. Today, company headquarters remain in Kansas while millions of their pizzas are sold around the globe. Many of them are ordered using telecommunications systems supplied by Sprint, whose world headquarters are near Kansas City. Nearby, Hallmark Greeting Cards employs Kansans, as do railroads, hospitals, food preparation plants, and the car manufacturer General Motors. "We have so much going on," says one computer technician, "I wish people didn't just think of Kansas and wheat!"

Mining plays a smaller role in the state's economy today than it once did. However, many oil and natural gas wells around the state

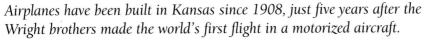

Airplanes have been built in Kansas since 1908, just five years after the Wright brothers made the world's first flight in a motorized aircraft.

are still pumping. The largest natural gas field in the nation is in southwestern Kansas near Hugoton. Helium, a gas used in balloons, underwater diving tanks, and computer semiconductors, is mined in southeastern Kansas.

Coal, limestone, and salt are also mined in Kansas. The largest salt mine in the state, in Hutchinson, is 650 feet straight down and forty-three football fields across. The mine has a surprising claim to fame: half a million boxes of important documents, microfilm, and other treasures are stored in the spaces where the salt has been excavated. At a constant sixty-eight degrees, the mine's conditions are perfect for preserving these items. The vault is "a favorite with all the major Hollywood studios," says Lisa Rarick, who works for the Hutchinson Salt Mine. "Down in the mine, we have the original negatives of thousands of films. Some are priceless, like *The Wizard of Oz* and *Gone with the Wind*." Making a film archive out of a hole in the ground is just one more example of how Kansans turn the ordinary into the extraordinary.

Most of Kansas's natural gas comes from the vast Hugoton gas field, which lies beneath eight counties.

4 PRAIRIE SPIRIT

Kansans can say they are from eastern Kansas or western Kansas. Or they can say they hail from the city or from the country. But no matter how they define themselves, Kansans generally agree on one thing—where they come from, people are friendly. "I'm just a Kansas girl," says businesswoman Leslie Hargis, "and whenever I go to New York or Chicago, I forget you aren't supposed to smile and wave at everybody. It's just that's what we do here!"

UNDER ONE BIG SKY

It is a misconception to think that everyone in Kansas lives on a farm. Most people live in or near Kansas City, Lawrence, Overland Park, Topeka, or Wichita. These cities offer all the cultural activities and high energy of any thriving American city.

Although most Kansans are urban dwellers, they are never totally removed from nature and agriculture. Even racing along the interstate through Kansas City or Topeka, drivers can hear crickets chirping above the sounds of traffic. Wild sunflowers bloom along the roadways in summer while turkey vultures circle overhead. Road signs remind travelers, "Every Kansas farmer feeds 128 people and YOU!"

Some Kansans worry that the small-town way of life might disappear.

SMALL-TOWN LIFE

Although Dorothy in *The Wizard of Oz* tells us that "there's no place like home," not every Kansas citizen is as pleased as she. "There's nothing to do," complains one young Dodge City salesperson. "There used to be a college here and interesting people came to town. Now, there's two new meatpacking plants and the college closed. You have to go to Garden City to do anything."

In western Kansas, the small cities that rely on cattle and oil are far removed from the diversity of bigger cities. "We're six hours to Denver, four hours to Amarillo, Texas, and we're closer to Oklahoma City than Topeka," says Rosalee Phillips, longtime resident of Liberal. "We can always go to the big city, but it's nice to live away from the hustle and bustle."

POPULATION GROWTH: 1870–2000

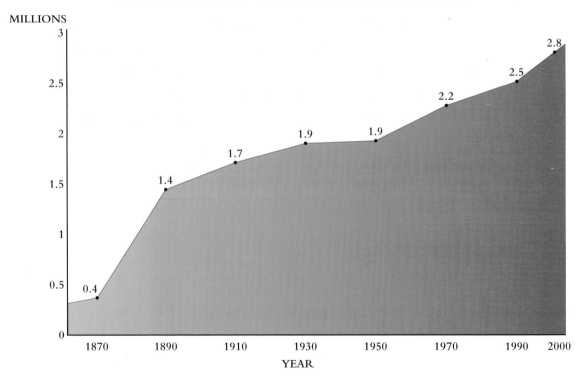

Many young people who go away to college don't come back. Between 1990 and 1995, ten thousand more people left the state than moved in. People in some rural communities are afraid their towns' populations will continue to dwindle. It worries those who are content to live where there are no malls, streetlights, or movie theaters. "Some of our towns are really dying," says one Hodgeman County resident.

But Jetmore's Nancy Ferguson-Moyer believes small-town life will always have its allure. Although many people move to the city for school or jobs, after they have families, the cities seem too intense; they want to come back home. "There's maybe only two houses for sale a year here, and they sell right away. We all want our backyards and our frontyards and to be able to see the sky!"

"Yes, it is a great place to live," agrees another Jetmore resident. "We are all connected. Weddings, graduations, football games, funerals, church suppers, everybody goes to everything! When there's a real big wedding, the people in the John Deere building clear all the tractors outside so we can have the wedding dance in their showroom!"

CELEBRATIONS ON THE PLAINS

It was a melting pot of Germans, Swedes, Swiss, Russians, Czechs, English, Scots, and Irish who first found their way to the Kansas prairie. They were encouraged by the railroads, which advertised all over northern Europe that inexpensive farmland was available in Kansas. The towns they settled and the holidays they celebrate show off their beginnings. Among the observances are the Swedish Saint

"We love living out here," says Nancy Ferguson-Moyer of Jetmore. "Everyone pulls together."

Swedish-American folk dancers show off their talents in Lindsborg.

The Cathedral of the Plains dominates the skyline in Victoria.

PANCAKE DAY

Each February, everyone in the Kansas cattle town of Liberal comes out for the traditional celebration of Pancake Day.

Pancake Day, you ask? "It's a very unique festival," says Liberal's Rosalee Phillips.

The story goes all the way back to 1445 in Olney, England. One morning, a woman was making pancakes when she heard the church bells ring. In her haste to get to church, she dashed out of the house still wearing her headscarf and apron. She arrived on time, skillet in hand. And so Olney's Pancake Race was born.

About five hundred years later, the citizens of Liberal proposed an international competition. Women in Olney and Liberal run a 415-yard, S-shaped course wearing dresses, aprons, and headscarves while carrying a skillet with a pancake. They have to flip the pancake at the start and the finish. Reports Mrs. Phillips, "It's an all-out sprint, but if they cross the finish line without that pancake, they're out of the race! I always encourage the ladies to keep their thumb on it!" Three runners share a race record of 58.7 seconds.

So it is that a fifteenth-century British legend is kept alive in Kansas, where twenty thousand townspeople and five thousand visitors get together to attend races, eat a pancake breakfast, and hear bagpipes play "Amazing Grace." "People call us from all over the world, asking about our race," says Rosalee Phillips. "It gives you goosebumps."

Thousands of Mennonites live in Kansas.

Lucia Day in Lindsborg, the Scottish Fest in McPherson, and Victoria Days, a Catholic German celebration held near the Cathedral of the Plains, a mammoth limestone church in north-central Kansas.

Opposed to slavery and war and believing in a simple, charitable life, many Mennonites fled Russia in the 1870s, when Czar Alexander II insisted they join the army. Thousands of Mennonites came to the United States; ten thousand alone immigrated to Kansas. Many Kansans today share a Mennonite heritage of hard work and generosity. Every year at the Mennonite Relief Auction, handcrafted

ETHNIC KANSAS

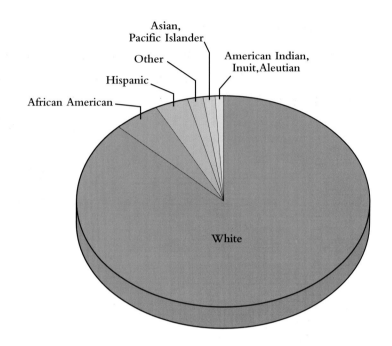

Asian,
Pacific Islander

Other

American Indian,
Inuit, Aleutian

Hispanic

African American

White

items, especially their world-famous quilts, are sold to benefit the poor.

One smaller Mennonite group, the Amish, settled near Yoder. Following stricter beliefs, the Amish avoid being too worldly by living without electricity and farming much the way early pioneers did. "Just look where the power lines don't go," says Yoder resident Kathryn Troyer, "that will be an Amish farm. Be careful driving, too, their horses and buggies go right down the middle of the road." Ask anyone in the state about Yoder and eyes roll up as stomachs are patted. "Oh, Yoder," everyone says, "the food the Amish make is *so* good!"

In the early twentieth century, immigrants from Mexico began settling in Kansas. Today, at 4 percent of the state's population,

Latinos are a well-established and growing group. Recently, Kansas City was voted among the top ten places to live by *Hispanic* magazine. In Garden City, the Mexican Fiesta in September has been celebrated with parades, dances, and piñatas for more than seventy-five years. "It's huge," says one resident. "People come from all over the country."

Since the 1970s, Southeast Asians from Cambodia, Laos, and Vietnam have been settling in Kansas. At that time, meatpacking

Kansas has a growing Latino population. Here, Topekans celebrate their Mexican heritage at the Fiesta Mexicana parade.

1-2-3-4 CAKE

This traditional cake is a Kansas farm kitchen favorite. It's as easy to remember as 1-2-3-4!

1 cup butter
1 teaspoon vanilla extract
2 cups sugar
4 teaspoons baking powder
3 cups flour
1 teaspoon salt
4 eggs
1 cup milk

Preheat oven to 350.

Blend the butter and sugar until the mixture is fluffy. Add eggs one at a time, beating after each. Stir in vanilla. Beat some more.

In another bowl, sift flour, baking powder, and salt together. Stir a little of the flour mixture into the butter/sugar mixture. Then add a little milk to the butter/sugar mixture and stir. Repeat, taking turns stirring in flour and milk little by little until everything is combined (about five turns).

Pour batter into an 8" x 13" baking pan that has been greased and floured. Bake 25 to 30 minutes.

Frost with any icing you like, or maybe just try jam!

"City or country, we feel close to our neighbors," says one resident of Central Kansas.

plants in rural areas were suffering a shortage of workers. Anxious to find work in their adopted country, Southeast Asians left California to fill the factory jobs in Kansas. Today, 8 percent of the population of Garden City, in southwestern Kansas, is Southeast Asian. Shop signs are written in Vietnamese and Cambodian as well as in Spanish and English. Celebrations such as Tet, the Vietnamese New Year, have brought a rich and diverse atmosphere to the Old West.

Only 6 percent of Kansans are African American, but you would never guess it from how many people attend "Homecoming" in the tiny town of Nicodemus. It is the "only all-black town west of the Mississippi," says local historian Angela Bates-Tompkins. The town was homesteaded by ex-slaves after the Civil War and blossomed in the 1870s and 1880s. But the High Plains were a harsh land, and the former slaves had few resources beyond their capacity for hard work, so when the railroad that was supposed to pass by was never built, the town faded. Today, its population is only thirty-five, but "thousands of descendants from all over the country come to Homecoming," says Bates-Tompkins. "We have food, crafts, and a dance Friday and Saturday nights. There's a gospel extravaganza, church on Sunday with a community dinner afterward. Everybody brings something to share, and that's the way it's always been." In 1998, the town of Nicodemus became a national historic site.

Although more than twenty-five Indian tribes have made their home in Kansas at one time or another, today less than 1 percent of Kansans are Native American. Most tribal groups once from the area now live in Oklahoma. One area where the Native American population is evident is in Lawrence, home of Haskell Indian Nations University, the only four-year Native American college in the country. The college has eight hundred students from 163 tribes. Ceremonies, powwows, and art markets are held on the school grounds, and the public is welcome to enjoy the displays of modern and traditional Native American life.

Not every festival in Kansas is connected to a particular ethnic group. Many festivals, such as the Wild Bill Hickok Rodeo and the John Brown Jamboree, celebrate frontier and western life. Pony Express Days commemorates the eighteen months that Pony Express

THE HAWK AND HIS FOUR DOGS: A WICHITA TALE

The Wichita tamed dogs to help with hunting and farm chores. Many of their legends honor their dogs as allies and companions. Here is one.

Once a chief's son had four dogs, one white, one red, one black, one copper. He kept them tied near his grass lodge. The boy had special powers, and the dogs were his guardians. One day the boy went out walking. He met two beautiful women wearing buffalo-hide robes. They traveled together until they approached a herd of buffalo. Then suddenly the women transformed into buffalo and began attacking the boy.

The boy tried to use his special powers to escape the snorting and stamping Buffalo-Women. He called upon other creatures such as the eagle to help him escape, but they could not.

Back at home his loyal dogs began barking furiously. The boy had asked his parents to unleash the dogs if they ever began barking. So the chief and his wife cut the ropes from the dogs' necks. The dogs raced to the boy's rescue and chased the buffalo away. However, the four faithful animals never returned home. Saddened by the loss of their companions and fearful of living without their protection, the boy and his family became hawks and flew away.

riders delivered mail from St. Joseph, Missouri, to Sacramento, California. The original Pony Express riders responded to ads that read, "Wanted. Young, skinny, wiry fellows. Not over 18. Must be expert riders. Willing to risk death daily. Orphans preferred. Pay $100 per

month." The riders galloped at top speed across Kansas, getting a new horse every ten to fifteen miles. Today, races are held at the site of one of the remaining Pony Express stations.

Kansans take great pride in their history and their place in the heart of the heartland. Their festivals honor the past and salute the future.

Kansas is home to more than twenty thousand Indians.

5 TO THE STARS

"Some places have the ocean," declares art professor Cima Katz, "but in Kansas the clouds are our ocean." Whether inspiration comes from overhead or otherwise, some Kansans reach for the sky and go beyond the ordinary.

HAVEN ON THE PLAINS

A simple thirteen-bed clinic on a twenty-acre Kansas farm has evolved into a hospital, school, and research center famous around the world. In 1920, Dr. Charles Menninger, a general practice physician, began a mental health clinic in Topeka. His two sons, Karl and Will, later became psychiatrists, and together they created a whole new way to treat patients.

After World War II, the Veterans' Administration put out an urgent call for more trained psychiatrists. Deeply troubled soldiers were returning from war, but there weren't enough doctors who knew how to treat them. To help, the father and his two sons established the Menninger School of Psychiatry. Right away, their school became the largest in the nation. They taught doctors to concentrate on caring for patients. As Dr. Karl Menninger has said, "Love cures people—both the ones who give it and the ones who receive it." Today, the Menninger Clinic is one of the world's leading psychiatric facilities.

Topeka's Menninger family gives the community credit for its success. "My father had an idea and an ideal, my brother and I worked at it, but everybody helped develop it," Karl Menninger said. "We have . . . . a wonderful American town."

RENAISSANCE MAN

For a full understanding of the term *Renaissance man*, you might look in Webster's Dictionary. It would describe a person capable of "vigorous, wide-ranging artistic and intellectual activity." Better still, you might read about the life of Gordon Parks.

The youngest of fifteen children, Gordon Parks was born in 1912 in Fort Scott, Kansas, an impoverished prairie town. His mother died when he was fifteen, but her wisdom and resistance to racism stayed with Parks his entire life. Parks grew up believing it was his duty to fight discrimination. His weapon was a camera.

In 1942, Parks found himself in Washington, D.C., with a remarkable job. He was hired to photograph people hard hit by the Great Depression. One of his first photographs, called *American Gothic*, became instantly famous. The original *American Gothic* is a painting by Grant Wood showing a resolute white farm couple

Gordon Parks once said that he used his camera as a "weapon against poverty and racism."

standing in front of a barn holding a pitchfork. Gordon Parks's *American Gothic* is a photograph of Ella Watson, a black cleaning-woman who worked in his office building. She posed holding a mop and a broom in front of an American flag. Nowhere else had Parks experienced the bigotry that he found in the nation's capital, and he wanted to express how he felt "about America and Ella Watson's position inside America."

His powerful photographs soon landed him a job with *Life* magazine. Parks traveled the world, photographing the beautiful and the exotic, but he never stopped documenting the lives of the unknown. In 1961, Parks published photos of an orphan named Flavio DaSilva who lived on the dirty streets of Rio de Janeiro, Brazil. Flavio was dying of tuberculosis. Parks urged Americans to remember the misfortunes suffered by others. Committed to his beliefs, Parks did more than just take Flavio's picture. He also brought him to the United States for a cure.

Parks wrote a book about growing up in Kansas called *The Learning Tree*, which he later made into a film. Then, in 1971, he directed *Shaft*, a film about a black detective, becoming the first African American to direct a major studio motion picture. Responsible for fifteen books, eight films, and countless photographs, Parks has also composed symphonies, cofounded the magazine *Essence*, and written a ballet about Martin Luther King Jr. In the 1990s, he began making art using computers.

To accomplish all this, Parks had to overcome poverty and racial hatred. He declares, "The anger and bitterness are there, but you use those emotions to help you do what you want to do." And he has done the extraordinary.

ROOM TO RUN

One icy winter morning in 1916, Glenn Cunningham and his brothers and sister arrived at their one-room schoolhouse in Rollo, Kansas. They set to building a fire while waiting for their teacher and schoolmates. But someone had replaced the can of starter fuel with a can of gasoline. As Glenn's brother poured gas onto the hot coals, the schoolhouse ignited. The children were horribly burnt; Glenn's legs were badly charred. His family nursed him devotedly, while doctors told them he would never walk again.

But Glenn, with the perseverance so common in pioneer families, pushed himself to the limits. Once he began walking again, his parents drew him out to the fields to chase rabbits for the dinner table. Moving was painful for Glenn, but his father would say, "Don't complain. Just try. Keep tryin'. You'll never catch a rabbit if you don't try." With that "never quit" philosophy, Glenn learned to outrun rabbits. He also learned to outrun track and field champions.

Glenn won his first track race as a fourth grader competing against high school boys. In college, he set a record for the world's fastest mile that went unbroken for nine years! But Cunningham wanted to do more, saying, "Someday I'd like to do something that would let the whole world know how much I love our country. Where else could a poor farm kid have the chance to do the things I've done?" So Cunningham joined the U.S. Olympic team. He came in fourth in the 1500 meter race in 1932. Four years later, he won the silver medal. Losing the gold medal pained Cunningham, but to every other American, his great spirit and determination was reason enough for the nickname the Iron Man of Kansas.

Drawn by miles of open space, many Kansas athletes excel at running. Jim Ryun is another. He made the U.S. Olympic team in 1964 while still a teenager in Wichita. That year, he became the first high school student in the world to run the mile in under four minutes. As patriotic as Cunningham, Ryun desperately wanted to win Olympic gold for his country. In 1968, he won the silver medal in the 1500 meter race. At the 1972 games he collided with another runner and did not qualify. Disappointed, Ryun said, "Everybody at some time has a fall. It's not so much the fall, it's what you do after the fall that matters—how you carry yourself. . . . Instead of it

Jim Ryun went from being a star athelete to serving as a U.S. congressman.

being a life-ending experience, it's been a life-enriching experience."
In 1996, Jim Ryun ran another race, and this time won. He proudly
serves Kansas as a U.S. representative.

   Some Kansas natives have brought Olympic gold home. In 1984,
Wichita's Lynette Woodard led the U.S. women's basketball team to
a gold medal. A year later, she was the first woman to play for the
Harlem Globetrotters, an elite African-American basketball team who
entertain while they play. After two years of dazzling fans with the
Globetrotters, she began playing in Japan. There she discovered
the business world, so she returned home and became a stockbroker

Lynette Woodard dominated women's college basketball during her four years at the University of Kansas.

on Wall Street. But basketball eventually lured her back onto the court. As one of the oldest members of the Women's National Basketball Association, Woodard began playing for the Detroit Shock. "We all love Lynette!" says one Kansan.

BORN TO LEAD

Few persons have had more influence on Kansas than two of its favorite sons: former Senate majority leader Bob Dole and former president Dwight D. Eisenhower. Overlooked, however, is another

Former Senate majority leader Bob Dole grew up in Russell, Kansas.

During his term as vice president, Charles Curtis practiced what he called "Americanism," which was praise for women, families, education, the separation of church and state, and fair labor practices.

favorite son, Charles Curtis, the only Native American vice president.

Born in 1860 to an English father and a French and Kaw mother, Curtis lived with his grandmother on Kaw tribal lands. One day, the Cheyenne raided the Kaw, and Charles's grandmother sent him by horseback to warn those up the creek. Clinging bareback to his horse, Charles decided he should also warn those in Topeka. His father lived in Topeka, so Charles stayed.

By the early 1870s, with their tribal lands in Kansas being chipped away, the Kaw were on the verge of starvation. In 1874, the last of the Kaw left for Oklahoma. Charles Curtis was prepared to go along, but his grandmother urged him to stay in school.

At age twenty-one, Curtis became a lawyer. In 1893, he was elected to the U.S. House of Representatives. He was an avid supporter of Civil War veterans, farmers, women's rights, and the right of U.S. citizenship for Native Americans. He became a senator and then in 1928 was elected vice president under President Herbert Hoover. It was said that Vice President Curtis welcomed more visitors to his office than anyone else in Washington. Kansans proudly called him "Our Charley."

SOARING OVER THE PLAINS

Two of the most successful women in aviation called Kansas their home. They had very different talents, but they shared a lifelong enthusiasm for airplanes and flying.

Pilot Amelia Earhart was born in 1898 in her grandparents' stately home in Atchison. From the very first time she donned a helmet and goggles and seated herself in the open cockpit of a plane, Earhart knew she "had to fly." She soon became one of the best female pilots in the country. In 1928, she was asked to be the first woman to fly across the Atlantic. Earhart was given the title flight commander, but the plane's pilot and navigator were both men. The flight was a huge success, especially in boosting Amelia Earhart's popularity.

In the excitement over "the girl," as people called her, the pilot and navigator were virtually ignored. Earhart scoffed at the title commander, saying she was no more than a "sack of potatoes" on the flight. But gaining glory without earning it made Earhart determined to be hailed for her own accomplishments. She resolved to increase women's involvement in aviation. She called for more women to become pilots, organized air races for women, and helped establish an international female pilots organization, the Ninety-Nines.

By 1932, no one had flown the Atlantic solo since Charles Lindbergh had made the first historic flight. Amelia Earhart wanted to be next. Always the publicity seeker, Earhart left Canada for the British Isles on May 20, 1932, five years to the day after Lindbergh's flight. Concerned over fuel, she traveled light, carrying little more than soup, tomato juice, and smelling salts to stay awake. When she touched down, hoping her destination had been reached, she asked a startled farmer, "Where am I?" The farmer replied, "In Gallegher's pasture."

Gallegher's pasture, which happened to be in Northern Ireland, was exactly the right place for Earhart. With this flight, she had broken many records, having become the first woman to fly the Atlantic solo and the only person to have flown the Atlantic twice. She had also flown a longer nonstop distance than any other woman, and made record time in the crossing. Earhart was showered with awards. She was the first woman to receive the Distinguished Flying Cross, which she accepted from her fellow Kansan Vice President Charles Curtis.

Despite her success, Earhart was not finished with stunt flying, and she began making plans for what was to be her last flight. Along with her navigator, Fred Noonan, she left Miami, Florida, eastbound for Los Angeles, California, via the world, a journey of

"I have a feeling that there is just about one more good flight left in my system," Amelia Earhart said as she was preparing for her fateful flight around the world.

29,000 miles. But with only 7,000 miles to go, their plane vanished over the South Pacific. Their disappearance is, to this day, a mystery.

Olive Ann Beech, on the other hand, kept her feet firmly on the ground. What she chose to pilot was her company. She and her husband, Walter Beech, founded the Beech Aircraft Company in Wichita in 1932. During the early days of aviation, people were just getting used to the speed and convenience of the automobile. They never thought airplanes would be a quick and easy way to travel. But the Beeches had a dream. They built a plane called the Staggerwing and entered it in a coast-to-coast race. Olive Ann Beech wanted

"I would say I was very fortunate throughout my life that I didn't have to do anything I didn't like," says Olive Ann Beech. "I enjoyed my life."

more than just to see the Staggerwing win. She wanted the win to be "spectacular." So she arranged to have a female pilot, Louise Thaden, who was also from Wichita, fly the race. The Staggerwing beat the second plane by a full half hour.

After Walter Beech grew ill in 1940, Olive Ann Beech ran the company for fifty more years. She steered Beech Aircraft a long way away from the days of the Staggerwing, eventually merging it with the Raytheon Aerospace Company. Beech's energy and great business sense helped her company grow from ten employees to ten thousand, causing many in the aircraft industry to call her the First Lady of Aviation.

CELLULOID CELEBRITY

Of the many film stars from Kansas, none is more recognized around the globe than the silent-film director and actor Buster Keaton. Born in hard times to unhappy and mismatched parents, Buster Keaton grew up making people laugh.

Myra and Joe Keaton's boy was born in Piqua, Kansas, in 1895. The Keatons were medicine show performers, who trouped from small town to small town hoping to con miners and farmers out of a few dollars. They neglected their child regularly, so it was no surprise that they often caught him falling into, out from, or off of something. The boy's resilience earned him the nickname Buster.

Though Myra was a trained musician, Joe had little talent. Few audiences found their act entertaining until the day Buster crawled out on stage. He drew more laughs than his parents ever had. So, from the tender age of four, he became the star of the show. Later, an adult Buster Keaton would sarcastically explain, "Before then, I was a burden to my parents." His parents billed their new act "The Boy Who Could Not Be Damaged." The act's highlight was Buster's father tossing and dragging him around stage. Buster's role was bouncing back, which he learned to do with great acrobatic skill.

Buster Keaton's sad face made the world laugh.

In Buster Keaton's first movie, *The Butcher Boy*, he backed onto the set tripping and falling and setting the stage for stardom. Soon, he was not only acting in movies, but directing them. His favorite, the movie he called his "pet," was *The General*. In this movie, Buster plays a Confederate train engineer during the Civil War. When Northern troops steal his beloved locomotive, Buster stops at nothing to get it back, even chasing after it down the railroad tracks riding an old-fashioned bicycle with a huge front wheel. Although a comedy, the movie, film buffs say, shows better than any other what America really looked like during the Civil War. They agree Buster Keaton's "pet" is a masterpiece.

6 HIGHWAYS AND TRAILS

By no means the largest state or the most populated, Kansas still has more miles of public roads than all but two other states. With 136,000 miles of highways, interstates, turnpikes, city streets, and rural byways, there are plenty of ways to explore the nooks and crannies of Kansas.

NATURAL WONDERS

While traveling westward across Kansas, you know you've reached the Flint Hills when rolling hills and farms give way to tallgrass prairie. "I've lived everywhere," says Cassoday waitress and steer roper Debbie Hoy, "but I always come back to the Flint Hills. It's a place where everything happens. And the animals—we have badger, possum, fox, mink, bobcats, deer, skunk, 'coons, wild turkey, prairie chickens, coyote, and now even armadillos are moving up." Roam the Tallgrass Prairie National Preserve and see and hear for yourself the hundreds of species of birds, insects, wildflowers, reptiles, and other animals. It is a walk worth taking, or better still, hitch up your saddle!

Natural Kansas is more than grasses. "You have to get out of your car and look," says biologist Nade Dangerfield. "The geology of Kansas is wild." The Monument Rocks National Landmark formations near Oakley in western Kansas are giant towers of chalk filled

Buffalo graze on the lush grasses of the Flint Hills.

with fossils from an ancient sea. You can find fossil remains of clams, oysters, sharks, fish, and flying reptiles. The nearby Fick Fossil and History Museum houses more than 11,000 sharks' teeth collected from the area! Not far down the road is Castle Rock, another chalk spire, which rises seventy feet straight up from the surrounding plain.

Near Ellsworth, in north-central Kansas, are the Mushroom

The chalk formations at Monument Rocks National Landmark tower sixty feet high.

Rocks. These huge sandstone formations look like orbs balanced on pedestals. Covering an area the size of two football fields, Rock City, outside of Manhattan, consists of more than two hundred rocks, some as big as houses. They were important (and startling) trail markers for the pioneers heading west. Go wander around. Rock City hasn't changed since it was formed millions of years ago.

PLACES TO SEE

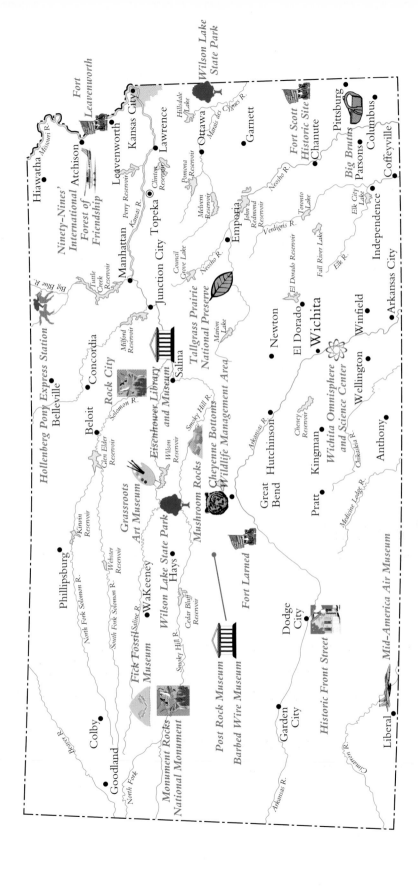

HITTING THE TRAIL

Kansas, by virtue of its central location, has long been a crossroads. Indians, explorers, traders, and settlers have traveled the length and breadth of the state, leaving behind their marks. Historic Kansas was covered in trails, and many modern roads follow those old trails.

Two towns along the Oregon Trail are particularly good stopovers. Atchison, the hometown of Amelia Earhart, has museums devoted to her life, but its most beautiful memorial to her is the Ninety-

TEN LARGEST CITIES

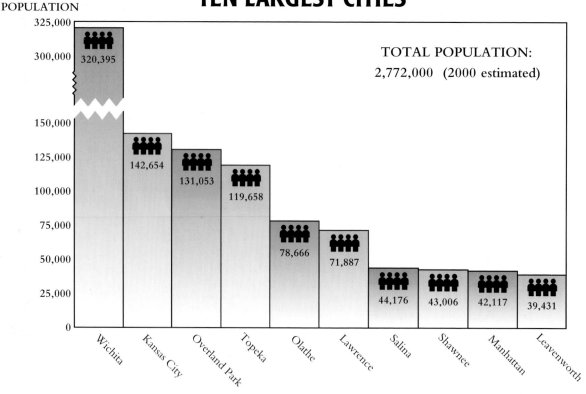

POPULATION

TOTAL POPULATION: 2,772,000 (2000 estimated)

- Wichita — 320,395
- Kansas City — 142,654
- Overland Park — 131,053
- Topeka — 119,658
- Olathe — 78,666
- Lawrence — 71,887
- Salina — 44,176
- Shawnee — 43,006
- Manhattan — 42,117
- Leavenworth — 39,431

Nines' International Forest of Friendship. The Ninety-Nines is an organization of female pilots from around the world. Earhart was their first president. She once wrote, "You haven't really seen a tree until you've seen its shadow from the sky." With this in mind, the Ninety-Nines built trails and gardens and planted trees representing all fifty states and dozens of countries. Stone markers honor pilots and astronauts such as Charles Lindbergh, Sally Ride, and the Wright Brothers. The start of a poem by Earhart borrows a line from an old hymn to describe the feelings stirred up by a visit to the Forest of Friendship, "Let there be peace on earth and let it begin with me."

Also along the old Oregon Trail is Leavenworth, Kansas's first city. The town is distinguished by Fort Leavenworth, the oldest active-duty army fort west of the Mississippi River, which was first established to guard a military road through Indian Territory. Probably the most famous federal prison in the country is in Leavenworth. Often called the Big House by lawbreakers, the massive building resembles the U.S. Capitol, complete with a silver dome on top. Architects designed the building to impress citizens with the grandeur of the law. Many notorious prisoners have called the Big House home, including gangsters Al Capone, Machine Gun Kelly, and the Bird Man of Alcatraz.

The longest trail through Kansas was the Big Lonely, or the Santa Fe Trail, which stretched all the way across Kansas. Today, Highway 50 follows the old trail. In places, wagon ruts are still visible.

Soldiers at Fort Larned protected traders along the trail. A walk through its buildings provides a taste of life on the frontier. Says visitor Cathy Bernard, "Look at the bullets they used. They look

THE BUFFALO SOLDIERS

Fort Leavenworth has had many notable officers, including President Dwight D. Eisenhower and former chairman of the Joint Chiefs of Staff Colin Powell. When General Powell was stationed at Leavenworth, he noticed that there was very little mention of the 9th and 10th Cavalry.

These two regiments were composed of African-American soldiers who fought in the Civil War. Afterward, many of them remained in the army. Because of their skin color, they were given the worst rations, horses, and assignments. They were ordered to protect settlers and stagecoaches from Indian raids, and despite their unfair treatment, they fought fiercely. Their loyalty and courage impressed even their foes, the Cheyenne. The Cheyenne respected them so much that they called them the Buffalo Soldiers, after their tribe's greatest symbol of bravery, the buffalo. The 9th and 10th Cavalry accepted the name as a badge of honor.

General Powell wanted to call the nation's attention to the Buffalo Soldiers and all the other African-American soldiers who have served in the U.S. military. He urged the government to build a memorial. The Buffalo Soldier National Monument now stands in Leavenworth. When it was dedicated in 1992, Powell declared that "the terrible over-looking of Black heroism in the military finally has ended."

like great, big round metal baseballs!" Nearby is the impressive limestone outcropping Pawnee Rock, where the Pawnee tribe held council meetings.

Looking nearly the same today as it did over a century ago, Council Grove is a lush river town brimming with a rich past. For many years the only trading post along the Santa Fe Trail, Council Grove was where travelers made last-minute repairs or gathered final supplies. The Osage and Kaw tribes signed a treaty with the U.S. government allowing the Santa Fe Trail to cross their lands.

At some places in Kansas, you can still see the ruts made by wagons traveling the Santa Fe Trail more than 150 years ago.

The treaty was signed under a tree known as the Council Oak. That tree still stands. So does the Post Office Oak, a tree with a large knothole where trail riders left each other mail.

THE WACKY KANSAS SPIRIT

Touring Kansas, you can't help but come face to face with the unexpected. "It's the wacky Kansas spirit," says historian Barbara Brackman. It can appear anywhere, at any time.

For instance, what would you do with a big hunk of outdated machinery? You would build a park around it, of course! At least, that's what the people of West Mineral decided to do. Driving through the heart of Kansas's mining country, you will see a mountain of steel looming on the horizon. This is "Big Brutus." At 160 feet tall and 11 million pounds, it is the second-largest electric mining shovel in the world. To reach layers of coal under the earth, huge pits were dug, and Big Brutus did the digging. He could fill three railroad cars with one giant scoop. By the 1970s, he was too expensive to run and too big to get rid of. Rather than allow his bulk to rust away, the people of West Mineral painted him orange and turned him into a museum. They let the pits surrounding him fill with water and stocked them with fish. Now, Big Brutus towers over visiting families while they fish, swim, and picnic. You can even climb the metal mountain. The view from the top is amazing!

Farther north, in La Crosse, you will find the Post Rock Museum

Until 1974, Big Brutus dug up the ground in search of coal.

and the Barbed Wire Museum. Post rock and barbed wire share a common past. When the pioneers first settled on the plains, they lived in fear of being trampled by marauding cattle. Without wood, they had no way to build fences. So when barbed wire was invented in the 1870s, the pioneers welcomed the chance to protect themselves. They carved fence posts from limestone, which they called post rock. Then they strung the prickly wire between the posts, successfully thwarting stampedes. As the museum guide explains, "Many people may dislike barbed wire, but we wouldn't be here without it!"

In the Barbed Wire Museum, you will see more than five hundred types of the "devil's rope." There are single strands and parallel strands, double knots and triple twists, as well as splicers and other tools used to twist and string it. Of particular interest to the less nimble-fingered is the display of old medicine bottles, with names like Glover's Barbed Wire Liniment: For Man & Beast. Post rock and barbed wire fences are still used all around this region. With no two stones exactly alike, the fences are wonderful to look at, but be careful. *Don't touch!*

For a truly different experience, drive past beautiful Wilson Lake State Park until you come to the whimsical town of Lucas. There, the Grassroots Art Center exhibits folk art made by midwestern artists. It features the art of Inez Marshall, who, though disabled, sculpted four-hundred-pound pieces of limestone into works such as a Model-T Ford with working headlights and a near-life-size covered wagon and mule team. Or walk a few blocks to Florence Deeble's house. A schoolteacher born in 1906, Deeble spent more than seventy years turning her backyard into a sculpture garden

Post rock fences are common in Central Kansas.

filled with concrete, crystals, and statues collected during her world travels. Walk a little farther and you will inevitably stop, quite abruptly, in front of S. P. Dinsmore's Garden of Eden.

A Civil War veteran, retired schoolteacher, farmer, and Populist politician, Samuel Perry Dinsmore was a character. Like Florence Deeble and Inez Marshall, Dinsmore expressed himself in limestone and concrete. In 1907, at age sixty-four, he began building his monument. First, he built a large three-story house of hand-chiseled

You can't miss S. P. Dinsmore's house in Lucas.

limestone made to look like a log cabin. Proud of his craftsman-
ship, Dinsmore opened his doors to passersby. As the first person in
town to have electric lights, he also saw the chance to make a little
money: he charged visitors a quarter to watch him switch the lights
on and off. People paid! Next, he spent twenty-two years building a
sculpture garden dedicated to his political and religious beliefs. He
sculpted 150 concrete statues as tall as his house. Among the figures
are Adam and Eve, the Devil, Lady Liberty, a banker, and even a
concrete American flag. It's quite a sight. If you are brave, there's

another sight—S. P. Dinsmore himself. He is preserved in a glass-topped coffin.

Dinsmore's Garden of Eden is irresistible. People have always stopped to stare. Dinsmore eventually erected a large steel and concrete sign over his garden gate. He said, "I could hear so many, as they go by, sing out, 'What is this?' so I put this sign up. Now they can read it, stop or go on, just as they please."

Perhaps S. P. Dinsmore could be speaking for all of Kansas. You can stop or go on, just as you please. But doesn't it seem better to stop?

THE FLAG: The Kansas flag consists of the state seal against a blue background. Below the seal is the word "Kansas." Above it is a sunflower, the state flower. The flag was adopted in 1927.

THE SEAL: The state seal, adopted in 1861, shows a landscape that includes a wagon train and two Indians hunting buffalo. In the foreground is a man plowing a field, which represents the importance of agriculture to the state. In the background is a steamboat on a river, symbolizing commerce. Above the scene are 34 stars, signifying Kansas's place as the 34th state.

STATE SURVEY

Statehood: January 29, 1861

Origin of Name: From the Kansa Indians, whose name means "people of the south wind"

Western meadowlark

Nickname: Sunflower State

Capital: Topeka

Motto: To the Stars through Difficulties

Bird: Western meadowlark

Flower: Sunflower

Tree: Cottonwood

Sunflower

HOME ON THE RANGE

In 1873, a prairie doctor named Higley Brewster of Smith County, Kansas, whose medical office and home was a typical sod house on the prairie, looked about and was moved by the beauty of the land. He was so over-whelmed that he wrote a poem, which when set to music by Daniel E. Kelly, became this most famous of all Western songs. It was adopted as the official state song in 1947.

Words by Higley Brewster   **Music by Daniel E. Kelly**

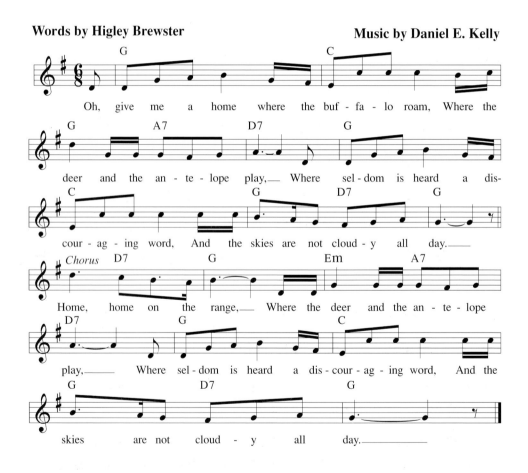

Insect: Honeybee

Animal: Buffalo

Reptile: Ornate box turtle

Amphibian: Barred tiger salamander

GEOGRAPHY

Highest Point: 4,039 feet above sea level, at Mount Sunflower

Lowest Point: 680 feet, along the Verdigris River in Montgomery County

Area: 82,282 square miles

Greatest Distance, North to South: 206 miles

Greatest Distance, East to West: 408 miles

Bordering States: Nebraska to the north, Missouri to the east, Oklahoma to the south, and Colorado to the west

Hottest Recorded Temperature: 121°F in Fredonia on July 18, 1936, and in Alton on July 24, 1936

Coldest Recorded Temperature: -40°F in Lebanon on February 13, 1905

Average Annual Precipitation: 27 inches

Major Rivers: Arkansas, Big Blue, Cimarron, Kansas, Missouri, Neosho, Republican, Saline, Smoky Hill, Solomon, Verdigris

Major Lakes: Cedar Bluff, Cheney, Fall River, John Redmond, Kanopolis, Kirwin, McKinney, Milford, Pomona, Toronto, Tuttle Creek, Webster

Trees: ash, black walnut, cottonwood, elm, hickory, locust, maple, oak, pecan, sycamore, willow

Wild Plants: aster, blue grama, bluestem, columbine, goldenrod, morning glory, sunflower, tumbleweed, verbena

Animals: beaver, coyote, muskrat, opossum, prairie dog, pronghorn, rabbit, raccoon, rattlesnake

Birds: blue jay, cardinal, crow, duck, hawk, meadowlark, pheasant, prairie chicken, quail, robin, sparrow, woodpecker

Fish: bass, bluegill, carp, catfish, crappie, walleye

Pronghorn

Endangered Animals: American peregrine falcon, black-capped vireo, black-footed ferret, Eskimo curlew, gray bat, Indiana bat, least tern, pallid sturgeon, Topeka shiner, whooping crane

Whooping cranes

TIMELINE

Kansas History

1500s The Kansa, Osage, Pawnee, Wichita, and Plains Apache Indians live in present-day Kansas

1541 Spaniard Francisco Vásquez de Coronado leads an expedition into Kansas in search of a legendary city of gold

1673 French explorers arrive in present-day Kansas

1803 Kansas becomes U.S. territory as part of the Louisiana Purchase

1821 The Santa Fe Trail is established from Franklin, Missouri, to Santa Fe, New Mexico, crossing Kansas

1827 Fort Leavenworth, the first U.S. outpost in present-day Kansas, is established

1830 Congress passes the Indian Removal Bill, forcing 27 tribes from the East into Kansas

1850s Violence erupts frequently over the issue of slavery, leading to the nickname Bleeding Kansas

1854 Land taken back from the Indians is opened to white settlement; Kansas Territory is created

1855 The territorial legislature provides for free schools for white children

1859 Kansas's first library opens in Vinland

1861 Kansas becomes the 34th state; the Civil War begins

1863 Most of Lawrence is burned by Confederate raider William C. Quantrill

Late 1860s Kansas towns such as Dodge City and Abilene become booming cow towns, shipping Texas longhorn cattle to other parts of the country

1870s Mennonite emigrants from Russia begin planting Turkey Red winter wheat, which soon becomes dominant in the state

1887 Susanna Madora Salter is elected mayor of Argonia, becoming the first female mayor in the United States

1892 Oil is discovered near Neodesha

1905 Helium is discovered near Dexter

1934–1935 Dust storms devastate Kansas farms

1941 The United States enters World War II

1952 Kansan Dwight D. Eisenhower is elected president

1954 The U.S. Supreme Court declares segregation in public schools illegal in *Brown* vs. *Board of Education of Topeka*

1986 Kansas voters approve a state lottery

1990 Joan Finney is elected the first female governor of Kansas

ECONOMY

Agricultural Products: beef cattle, corn, hay, hogs, milk, sorghum, soybeans, sugar beets, wheat

Corn seeds

Manufactured Products: airplanes, chemicals, farm equipment, food products, printed materials, railroad cars, rubber products

Natural Resources: coal, helium, limestone, natural gas, oil, salt

Business and Trade: banking, insurance, transportation, wholesale and retail trade

CALENDAR OF CELEBRATIONS

International Pancake Race Each February, women in Liberal compete against women in Olney, England, in this 415-yard footrace carrying a pancake on a skillet.

Wichita River Festival The people of Wichita take advantage of their beautiful May days with this festival that includes hot air balloons, evening concerts, and fireworks displays.

Wah-Shun-Gah Days Dancing, crafts, a Santa Fe Trail ride, and even an antique tractor pull are all part of the festivities at the Kaw powwow in Council Grove in June.

Twin Rivers Festival Emporia celebrates the arts in June with dances, concerts, arts-and-crafts displays, and lots of children's activities.

Beef Empire Days Beef is big business in Garden City. In June the town holds a festival that both educates and features fun events such as rodeos, a pancake feed, and a cowboy poetry reading.

Fiesta Mexicana Each July, Topeka's Mexican-American population puts on one of the largest Hispanic festivals in the Midwest. There is a parade, folk dancing, games, traditional foods, and even a jalapeño-pepper-eating contest for the brave.

Lenexa Spinach Fest Lenexa was once the largest spinach producer in the world. Each September, the town holds a festival honoring spinach, which includes the world's largest spinach salad (using 500 pounds of spinach), spinach milkshakes, spinach tortillas, and hats made out of vegetables.

Pioneer Days Hays remembers its pioneer past every September with demonstrations of skills such as rope making, whittling, and stone-post cutting.

Renaissance Festival Every weekend in September and October Bonner Springs holds a Renaissance Festival. Visitors munch on turkey drumsticks while jesters cavort and knights on horseback try to topple each other.

Renaissance Festival

Fall Festival North Newton honors its Mennonite past in October with a celebration that includes crafts, athletic competitions, and cooking demonstrations. Don't miss the verenike (cheese-filled pastries) or the New Year's cookies.

Lucia Fest Lindsborg welcomes the Christmas season with this traditional Swedish festival that features music, folk dancing, and lots of delicious Swedish baked goods. Its highlight is the crowning of St. Lucia, who wears a crown of candles.

STATE STARS

Annette Bening (1958–   ) is an actress best known for her Oscar-nominated performance as a smooth con artist in *The Grifters.* Bening began her career on the New York stage, earning a Tony nomination for her role in *Coastal Disturbances,* before turning her attention to film. An actress who radiates intelligence and elegance, Bening has appeared in a wide variety of movies, from *Mars Attacks!* to *American Beauty.* She was born in Topeka.

Annette Bening

Gwendolyn Brooks (1917–   ), a poet who was the first African American to win a Pulitzer Prize, was born in Topeka. Since the publication of her

poetry collection *A Street in Bronzeville* in 1945, she has been acclaimed for her intense and often witty depictions of black urban life. Brooks earned the 1950 Pulitzer Prize for *Annie Allen.*

Gwendolyn Brooks

William Burroughs (1914–1997) was a writer famous for his experimental novels, which often include grosteque imagery and dark humor. His best-known work, *Naked Lunch,* brilliantly depicts the paranoid and almost mad mindset of drug addicts. Born in Missouri, Burroughs lived much of his later life in Lawrence, Kansas.

Clyde Cessna (1879–1954), an airplane manufacturer, was born in Iowa and grew up in Kansas. For a while Cessna worked as an auto mechanic, but after seeing his first air show in 1910, he was hooked on planes, and he built his first plane that winter. In 1917, he became the first airplane manufacturer in Wichita, which had become a hub of aviation activity. Cessna eventually built the first plane in the country that had no struts or wires connecting the wings to the body. In 1927, he founded the Cessna Aircraft Company.

Walter Chrysler (1875–1940), an automaker, was born in Wamego and grew up in Ellis. Chrysler began his career as a railroad mechanic. He later worked for Buick and General Motors before founding the Chrysler

Corporation in 1925. It eventually became one of the world's largest automobile companies.

Buffalo Bill Cody (1846–1917) was a legend of the Wild West. He was born in Iowa, but his family soon became among the first pioneers to settle Kansas. Cody's adventures began early. At age fourteen, he became a Pony Express rider, and during the Civil War, he was a scout for the Union army. After the war, the Kansas Pacific Railroad hired him to provide buffalo meat for the crews laying track. Killing as many as 2,000 buffalo a month, Cody earned his nickname. In later years, Cody became famous as a showman, organizing the wildly popular Wild West Show, which presented a romantic view of life in the West.

Amelia Earhart (1898–1937), a native of Atchison, was a pioneering pilot. She was the first woman to fly across the Atlantic, the first woman to fly solo across the Atlantic, and the first person to fly solo across the Pacific. Her plane disappeared in 1937 while she was attempting to fly around the world.

Dwight D. Eisenhower (1890–1969) was the 34th president of the United States. Eisenhower was born in Texas and moved to Abilene, Kansas, as a baby. He attended West Point Military Academy and worked his way up through the army ranks to become a general. During World War II, Eisenhower commanded all Allied troops in Europe and accepted the German surrender. During his two terms as president, he ended the Korean War and began work on the interstate highway system, the largest construction project in history.

Dwight D. Eisenhower

Wild Bill Hickok (1837–1876) was a famous lawman of the Wild West. Hickok was born in Illinois and moved to Kansas at about age 18. He worked as a stagecoach driver on the Santa Fe Trail and served as a Union spy and scout during the Civil War. His first law enforcement job was in Monticello, Kansas. He later became a U.S. marshall in Fort Riley, Hays, and Abilene, gaining fame for bringing peace to these lawless towns. Hickok was eventually shot dead in a saloon in Deadwood, South Dakota.

Dennis Hopper (1936–   ) is an actor known for his rebellious, oftentimes crazed characters. He became widely known in 1969, when he wrote, directed, and starred in *Easy Rider*. This film, about a cross-country motorcycle trip, became a big hit and an emblem of the 1960s counterculture. Although Hopper occasionally directs movies, he has focused more on acting, appearing in such disturbing films as *Blue Velvet* and *River's Edge*. Hopper was born in Dodge City.

Langston Hughes (1902–1967) was an influential writer who gained prominence as part of the Harlem Renaissance, a flowering of the arts that took place during the 1920s in New York's most famous black community. Hughes is best remembered for his poems, such as "The Negro Speaks of Rivers" and "Harlem," which incorporate everyday language and the rhythms of black music. Hughes spent much of his childhood in Lawrence and Topeka. His novel *Not Without Laughter* describes his youth in Kansas.

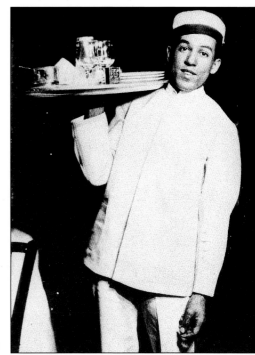

Langston Hughes

William Inge (1913–1973), a renowned playwright, was born in Independence and attended the University of Kansas. In plays such as *Bus Stop, Picnic,* and *Come Back, Little Sheba,* Inge explored the hopes and frustrations of people living in small towns. All of these plays were turned into films. Inge also wrote directly for the screen, most famously *Splendor in the Grass,* which earned him an Academy Award for Best Original Screenplay.

Walter Johnson (1887–1946) is considered by many to be baseball's greatest pitcher ever. Johnson, who was nicknamed Big Train because he threw so fast, was born in Humboldt. In his 20 years with the Washington Senators, he won 416 games, the second-highest total in baseball history. He threw 110 shutouts, a major league record, and led the American League in strikeouts 12 times. Johnson was elected to the Baseball Hall of Fame in 1936.

Walter Johnson

Nancy Kassebaum (1932–   ) was the first female U.S. senator from Kansas. The daughter of Alfred Landon, the governor of Kansas and the 1936 Republican presidential candidate, she was born in Topeka. In 1978, Kassebaum was elected to the U.S. Senate, becoming the first female senator elected to a full term who did not succeed her husband in either house of Congress.

Buster Keaton (1895–1966) was a silent film director and actor famous for his deadpan expressions and extraordinary timing and comic sense. In such masterpieces as *Sherlock, Jr., The Navigator,* and *The General,* Keaton played characters who could endure any frustration and were oblivious to danger. After the silent film era ended, Keaton's career declined, and he was forced to play minor roles. He was born in Piqua.

Carry Nation (1846–1911) was a leader in the movement to outlaw alcohol. Nation, who was born in Kentucky, was the widow of an alcoholic. She eventually settled in Medicine Lodge, Kansas, where she began giving lectures on the evils of liquor. She gradually became more radical and began destroying saloons with a hatchet. Though she was arrested 30 times, she inspired others to fight for Prohibition.

Sara Paretsky (1947–   ) is a mystery writer who created the strong, independent, and witty female private eye V. I. Warshawski. Paretsky's novels such as *Burn Marks* and *Blood Shot* are notable for being murder mysteries that also deal with social problems. Paretsky grew up in Lawrence.

Charlie Parker (1920–1955), a Kansas City native, was the greatest and most influential saxophone player of all time. Parker helped found the bebop style of jazz, which was fast, complex, and rhythmically inventive. To this day, saxophonists learning to play copy his improvisations. Parker, who was nicknamed Bird, is responsible for such classic songs as "Ornithology" and "Bird's Nest."

Charlie Parker

Gordon Parks (1912–   ) is a photographer, filmmaker, artist, writer, and composer. After gaining recognition for his photographs of poor people during the 1940s, Parks became prominent as a photographer for *Life* magazine. In 1971, he directed *Shaft*, becoming the first African American to direct a Hollywood motion picture. Parks was born in Fort Scott.

Gale Sayers (1944–   ) was one of the greatest running backs in football history. Sayers was born in Wichita and attended the University of Kansas, where his speed and dazzling moves earned him the nickname the Kansas Comet. During his rookie season with the Chicago Bears, he set a league record of 22 touchdowns and once scored a record six touchdowns in one game. Although his career was cut short by injury, he twice led the league in rushing. In 1977 at age 34, he became the youngest player ever inducted into the Pro Football Hall of Fame.

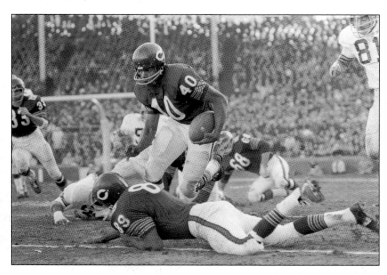

Gale Sayers

Rex Stout (1886–1975) was a writer who created Nero Wolfe, one of mystery's greatest detectives. Wolfe loves gourmet food and orchids and seldom leaves his house. Instead he sends his amiable, wiseguy assistant,

Archie Goodwin, to do the legwork. Stout, who wrote more than 40 Nero Wolfe books, grew up in Wakarusa.

Rex Stout

Clyde Tombaugh (1906–1997), an astronomer, was born in Illinois and later moved with his family to a farm in western Kansas. It was there, in 1925, that he built his first telescope. After studying the planets through another telescope he had made himself, Tombaugh took a job at Lowell Observatory in Arizona looking for a ninth planet in the solar system. In 1930, he discovered Pluto.

Lynette Woodard (1959–   ), a native of Wichita, is one of the best female basketball players of all time. At the University of Kansas, she broke 24 of the 32 records kept for women's college basketball, including scoring a record 26.3 points per game for her four years of college. Woodard later joined the comic but extremely talented Harlem Globetrotters, becoming the first woman ever to play professional basketball with men.

TOUR THE STATE

Historic Front Street (Dodge City) For a taste of the Old West, visit this reconstruction of two Dodge City blocks from the 1870s. You can walk down

Historic Front Street

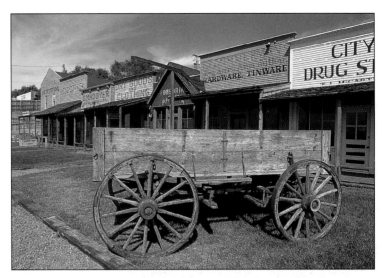

wooden sidewalks past a general store and a blacksmith shop and then step through the swinging doors of Long Branch Saloon.

Mid America Air Museum (Liberal) You'll get a close-up view of nearly 70 flying machines at this museum, including a 1929 Pietenpol, which is powered by a Model-A automobile engine.

Fick Fossil and History Museum (Oakley) In addition to thousands of sharks' teeth and other fossils, this museum displays cattle brands, a sod house, and railroad equipment.

Cathedral of the Plains (Victoria) This beautiful limestone church was built by German-Russian settlers in the early 20th century.

Garden of Eden (Lucas) Monumental concrete statues fill the yard of S. P. Dinsmore, who sculpted all the figures after becoming a senior citizen.

Wilson State Park (Russell) A region of rugged rock arches, steep barren hills, and deep canyons, this is the perfect place for hiking, fishing, boating, and picnicking.

Cheyenne Bottoms Wildlife Management Area (Great Bend) Wildlife lovers come from all over to visit the largest inland marsh in the United States, where nearly 15 million shorebirds spend the winter.

Rock City (Minneapolis) Large sandstone rocks rise from the prairie at this site. Some are almost perfectly round, others look like pyramids, and still others are balanced precariously atop one another.

Wichita Omnisphere and Science Center (Wichita) The highlight of this science museum is the planetarium's fascinating star show. You can also enjoy lots of hands-on exhibits covering such subjects as optical illusions and electricity.

Henry's Sculpture Hill (Augusta) As you drive down the highway east of Wichita, a giant grasshopper, eagle, and lion loom in the distance. If you stop in, you can view more than 100 sculptures created by Franklin Jensen.

Hollenberg Pony Express Station (Hanover) Built in 1857, this is the only unaltered Pony Express station that still stands on its original site.

Potwin Place (Topeka) Brick roads snake among the grand houses of this historic neighborhood.

Missouri River Queen (Kansas City) For a relaxing afternoon, take a cruise on the Missouri River in this turn-of-the-century paddle-wheel boat.

Old Depot Museum (Ottawa) Housed in an old railroad depot, this historical museum features a 1918 locomotive and exhibits on Bleeding Kansas and the Civil War.

Big Brutus (West Mineral) This 15-story-high orange mining shovel is now the centerpiece of a park filled with lovely lakes and picnic areas.

Fort Scott National Historic Site (Fort Scott) On a visit to this fort built in the 1840s, you can tour a hospital, officers' quarters, and a bakery.

FIND OUT MORE

There's a lot more to find out about Kansas. Ask for these titles at your library, a bookstore, or a video store. Don't forget to look on the Internet, too.

BOOKS

Alter, Judy. *The Santa Fe Trail.* Danbury, CT: Children's Press, 1998.

Chu, Daniel, and Bill Shaw. *Going Home to Nicodemus: The Story of an African American Frontier Town and the Pioneers Who Settled It.* Morristown, NJ: J. Messner, 1994.

Deitch, Kenneth M., and JoAnne B. Weisman. *Dwight D. Eisenhower: Man of Many Hats.* Lowell, MA: Discovery Enterprises, 1990.

Fradin, Dennis Brindell, and Judith Bloom Fradin. *Kansas.* Chicago: Childrens Press, 1995.

Janeczko, Paul B., ed., *Home on the Range: Cowboy Poetry.* New York: Dial Books, 1997.

MacLachlan, Patricia. *Sarah, Plain and Tall.* New York: Harper & Row, 1985.

Reef, Catherine. *Buffalo Soldiers.* New York: Twenty-First Century Books, 1993.

Rounds, Glen. *Sod Houses on the Great Plains.* New York: Holiday House, 1995.

Szabo, Connie. *Sky Pioneer: A Photobiography of Amelia Earhart.* Washington, D.C.: National Geographic Society, 1997.

VIDEOS AND RECORDINGS

The Buffalo Soldiers. Produced by Adrienne Armstrong; written and directed by Bill Armstrong. Bill Armstrong Productions, 1992.

Santa Fe Trail. Directed by Michael Curtiz. Santa Monica, CA: MGM/UA Home Video, [1993], 1940.

Tornado. Bethesda, MD: Discovery Communications, 1997.

Weed, Joe. *Prairie Lullaby* [sound recording]. Los Gatos, CA: Highland Records, 1993.

The Wizard of Oz. Culver City, CA: MGM/UA Home Video, 1991.

WEBSITES

There are many wonderful Kansas pages on the World Wide Web. Here are some of the biggest:

State Library of Kansas, Blue Skyways
http://skyways.lib.ks.us/kansas/

From Sea to Prairie: A Primer of Kansas Geology by Catherine S. Evans
http://www.kgs.ukans.edu/publications/primer/primer01.html

Kansas State Historical Society
http://www.kshs.org

Information Network of Kansas (the official state government site)
http://www.ink.org/

INDEX

Page numbers for charts, graphs, and illustrations are in boldface.